MW00834285

Psalm 105

"*Give thanks to the Lord, call on His name;*

> *make known among the nations what He has done.*

Sing to Him, sing praise to Him;

> *tell all of His wonderful acts.*

Glory in His Holy name;

> *let the hearts of those who seek the Lord rejoice.*

Look to the Lord and His strength;

> *seek His face always.*

Remember the wonders He has done,

> *His miracles and the judgements He pronounced.*

He is the Lord our God..."

NIV version. Verses 1 - 7

You Will Never Walk Alone: God Pursues Us

© 2019 by Gwendolyn Bell-Kameka

All Rights Reserved

Requests for permission to quote from this book should be emailed to gbellkameka@yahoo.com

This book is a non-fiction.   The names of people and business have been changed.   Names of my schools, relatives, teachers, and incidents that were in the news were not changed to preserve the authenticity of the stories. All stories are from my personal life as I recollect them and how they have impacted my life.

ISBN-13: 978-0-578-47726-8

YOU WILL NEVER WALK ALONE

God Pursues Us

GWENDOLYN BELL- KAMEKA

To Mama Bell, it started with you. Your unbelievable faith in the promises of God has opened the chapters to my personal walk in faith.

Elisa

You are the path that will lead others to the truth!

Elizabeth

CONTENTS

INTRODUCTION

Introduction

Dear Reader – You are loved more than you can imagine. Before you were born you were on the mind of the Creator. You were breathe into being and the Spirit of the Divine resides in you. Imagine that, the Creator of all that your eyes can behold lives within you.

The winds of life may have knocked you down making you feel alone, lost, hopeless, and you may even think that no one cares for you. I want you to read the pages of this book and see that even in your most difficult times your Creator is with you. The God who created the universe and all that is in it hovers over you.

This book is a personal account of my spiritual journey. As with most personal stories, some pieces were hard to write, they took me back to places of extreme hurt and pain; at only nine years old I saw a bullet hitting my classmate, I was 17 years old and 120 miles from home when my aunt put out in the rain, I watched as my husband's life was covered in question marks with a gun pointed at him, I have mourned miscarriages, and suffered in the silent rage of an undiagnosed illness. **The Sun Will Rise After the Rain, Ricochet, and There is Power in Prayer** were the most difficult for me to share.

I also had so much joy writing this book for you. I am excited for you to see that there is joy on the other side of sorrow and there is peace where you thought only pain exists. In all these stories there is the restorative, redemptive love of God. God uses nature, revelations in dreams, human interactions, and sometimes the voice within to reveal His goodness. What happens to a miscarriage when a father prays? Can the name of Jesus stop a bullet? Is it possible that the Creator hears the cries of hungry children and provide food from the sky? And does God care for prisoners?

God is not sitting on the pages of the Bible but is active and alive, stitching together the pieces of your life to make a beautiful picture. God has great plans for your life, you were created for mighty works. The things that were meant for evil, God will use them to promote you and bless you.

You may question these stories, how can they be true? There are stories in this book that will have you asking, who is this God? These are my experiences and to be authentic I had to write all of it, the beautiful parts, and the painful bits. This is my life, unbelievable but true.

The God that I learned about as a child is one who sits in heaven with a large book writing down all the wrongs that I have ever done and is waiting for an opportunity to say, "Got you!" But that is contrary to the God that I got to know personally and the God I want you to know.

You may carry the scars of your past but be sure to know that God can heal all wounds. You are not the wrongs that you have done, you are love and light, you are the perfect love of the Creator.

And remember, **YOU WILL NEVER WALK ALONE**

"Gwen Kameka is a very talented storyteller. Her stories had me holding my breath and then boom! God's grace came showering down. A true testament of the power of faith."

Dr. Howard E. Kea, Behavioral Scientist & Life Coach

"There are so many lessons in this one book: faith, belief, resilience, fight, appreciation, poverty, confidence, care, broken heart, love, miracles, family values, strength, team work, and more. You will definitely miss out on how amazing this thing called life can be if you didn't read this book. Thank you Gwendolyn Bell-Kameka. Thank you.

Patrick Green, Author, Entrepreneur, & Journalist

God Heals

Jehovah Rapha

Jehovah Heals - He will heal the bitter waters of this life
"...For I am the Lord who heals." **Exodus 15 verse 26**

1. Miscarriages Restored
2. A 12 Year Mystery Solved
3. Prescription from Heaven

1

Miscarriages Restored

"And he said, about this season, according to the time of life, you will have a son. And she said, No, my lord, you are a man of God, do not lie to your servant. And the woman conceived and had a son at that season that Elisha had said unto her, according to the time of life." 2 Kings 4 verses 16-17.

The fetal heart monitor echoed silence. Dr. Black searched the ultrasound machine for signs of life, and the dark screen returned blank stares. The silence was becoming a routine for me, but routine didn't dull the insidious pain that pierced my heart. Nothing could hide our pain, not even the thick black drapes that were drawn across the glass window panes. Our sorrow filled every vacant space in the doctor's office, draining the air we breathed. My husband, Mark, and I could recite the doctor's monologue, "I am sorry; there is no fetal pole." Mark and I have felt the heavy blow of those eight words three times before, and the fourth would be no easier to bear. How many times can my heart break before it dies?

******

Jehovah Rapha – God Heals

Truthfully, children were never in my plans, not because I did not like them, that is far from it: as early as age ten, I took the children in my neighborhood, combed their hair, bathed them, fed them, and taught them to read. However, premature death and the harshness of the ghetto corroded the glow of the children around me; swallowing them along with their dreams. Too many empty spaces in my classroom after a holiday break – James Stone drowned in the river during the summer of 1979, and Donna Shorty killed by her stepfather that same year on Christmas day.

At only nine years old I lost my innocence standing in the middle of a gun battle at my school. I witnessed the exchange of gunshots between the principal's wife, Mrs. Spence, and a gunman who came to rob the school in the glare of noonday. Thick, red blood flowed at my feet, the tiny lifeless body of my classmate slumped on the hot concrete where I was playing just a minute before.

The day of the funeral, my classmates and I practiced the song that we were going to sing at the church service in her honor one last time – 'When He cometh to take up His Jewels'. I left the rehearsal confused by the words of the song, 'All the pure ones, all the bright ones. His love and His own'. I learned in Sunday School that God loves me. If God only took those whom he loves and the ones who are good and pure, I might be next on His list.

After the rehearsal, I went home to change out of my school uniform and into good church clothes. I slumped on the hot concrete step in my backyard. Cold sweat washed

Jehovah Rapha – God Heals

over me, and the blazing afternoon sun could not warm the chills and shivers I felt inside my body. My tummy cramped until I curled my body into a ball, my legs ached. I lay on the step and slept until the cool of the evening when Mama came home, and I heard her calling my name. I didn't ask about the funeral when I returned to school, and no one asked how this death affected the children who witnessed that gruesome day.

I carried the pains from the empty classroom benches and the decay of unfilled promises with me; each loss filled up the spaces where little girls dreamed of motherhood. How much pain does it take to stop wanting?

As I peeled back the curtains to my childhood, I also saw the mammoth task and drudgery of raising children. My position as the middle child in a large family of nine gave me a bird's eye view of my family's lives, and it all looked to be no more than perfect chaos.

My brothers came home from football games with sprained ankles, and broken toes and Mama had to put them back together. My siblings were skilled in finding trouble and incompetent in getting out of it. There was never enough food to eat, and we fought for sleeping space. My sisters went off to parties without permission and never finished their chores leaving behind mountains of laundry and unswept floors. Dada was always searching for children who stayed out too late.

The hardships of the ghetto broke me in several pieces, and I covered the gaping wounds with fear. Fear caused me to cry spontaneously whenever a baby was born. I know that this perfect child getting all the attention and wearing new clothes dusted in baby powder would soon be running around fending for himself.

Excessive focus on one aspect of life can create myopic degeneration, and I declared motherhood was never for me. I was so firm in that decision that at eight years old when I got a doll for Christmas, I threw it in the pit latrine. I was not even going to play mommy to a doll.

******

Right out of college I met the love of my life. In 1989 Mark was a skinny guy with thick, curly, chestnut hair, and hazel eyes. He caught me off guard with his crooked smile and his bright humor. Mark was nothing like the boys in my neighborhood. His love and laughter filled my broken places.

He is humble, tender, loving, and everything he touches comes alive. To watch him with children, animals, and plants is a thing of beauty.

But...

A 'but' always shows up when a good thing is about to happen. 'Buts' can derail the best plans and we had our fair share. Our first, the bitter fight with his parents; I can't tell you the details now, but there was a 'but' about color. Then the 'but' about children; he wanted plenty and I wanted zero.

Mark's dreams were different from mine. My priority was to run away from poverty, that meant no children. I

Jehovah Rapha – God Heals

wanted the freedom to run from hardships should I see it coming my way. I've often listened to the ladies in my community reminiscing about the things they didn't achieve, and they placed their losses squarely on their children's shoulders –

"If me neva have dem pickney ya, me wudda gone bout me business and live a betta life."

Another would chime in –

"No true?" "Me cudda guh a Kingston go find gud wuk, but de pickney dem tie me dung."

I didn't want to be the women from my community. I didn't want to be tied down. I wanted options for myself. I craved survival. Mark, on the other hand, came without the worries that held me hostage. He wanted children, plenty children. He didn't want to run away from anything or anyone; he wanted to settle down. Mark wanted to thrive.

******

I had slipped too deep into love and was crazy for him, too late to turn back now. I wanted to be his wife more than my fear of motherhood and decided to give him the only gift he wanted, children.

We planned on having four children, not eight - his starting point. If things turned out the way we had expected, our babies would be two years apart. In 1991, our first, an 8lbs 12 oz. girl who turned out to be a precocious, bossy, but brilliant big sister. Then in 1993, we had our only son. He was 7.5lbs, and as a baby, he cried by the tick of the clock, he grew up to be a courageous, and protective brother.

Our home was alive and filled with joy. You could often find us at home singing along and dancing to Celine Dione, Kenny Rogers, Anita Baker, Cocoa Tea, Gregory Issacs, and other well-known R&B, Country, and Reggae artists. We played card games, chess, and solved large picture puzzles. And there were nightly readings of bedtime stories with the children. Everywhere Mark went, except for work, you would see all four of us. We went to the beach, took long rides across the winding roads to the country, visited game rooms where we played pool and threw darts.

Motherhood grew on me, and my heart expanded from only loving Mark to pouring my heart into these two tiny human beings. I was tied to them, and I was happy. As I watched the ease with which Mark cared for our children and his fierce protectiveness for them I no longer feared that they would be lost to the world that would snatch their dreams from them. Their hopes and dreams would be theirs to carry. Sometimes the things we need to grow are the things we fear most. When we let go of fear, there is so much joy waiting for us on the other side.

******

Two years after my son was born, we tried for baby number three. Eight weeks into that pregnancy, we mourned our first loss. Outwardly, I blamed this loss on my heavy work schedule and the stress of purchasing our first home. But to be honest, I blamed myself. If I had taken better care of myself... if only I had positive thoughts... if I had done things differently...I could have carried this baby to full term. No one blamed me, and no one needed to, my recrimination took its toll. We tried again and again, and all three pregnancies ended in a miscarriage at eight weeks. Each spotting and subsequent visit to my obstetrician tore our hearts out. I was slowly slipping to the edge.

Looking back, I can see how sadness and pain created a wall too tall to climb and cast a shadow so wide it left me in depression. My marriage was dying, and my home was becoming a graveyard. Muted conversations replaced our singing, and we fussed over the slightest misunderstanding. The pain I carried because of these miscarriages might not be the truth for all women. For me, the inability to bring forth life when I planned it made me feel useless.

I questioned God: "God are you punishing me for never wanting children?" "God am I being punished for past sins?" I drifted from God and my family, and I found respite in work, and friendships that would prove destructive. Drifting is an unintentional act and will lead to unintended consequences.

Some people may ask, "What was your problem? You already had two children." It never matters how many children I had, every miscarriage felt like an ocean of pain with skyscraper waves that keep crashing down. I cannot fully explain it - but the very moment I knew I was carrying a child I started to build a connection with the hope of how

Jehovah Rapha – God Heals

this child would shape the future and erase the pains of my past.

We gave up. No... I gave up. I was going to be happy as a family of four.

******

In the summer of 2000, two years after our third miscarriage, we got a new dining table made to seat six people. Without thinking, I blurted out, as if speaking to the wind –

"I would love to fill out this dining table."

All four of us busted out laughing at the ridiculousness of the idea of having more children. My son, the baby, was almost eight years old.

During that time, a friend of mine, Janet Robinson, who was recently married, was trying to have a child with no success. Every morning before we started our work I would sit with Janet and pray with her for the Divine to give her a baby. We did this for a few months, but nothing changed.

Two months later, in October, after my wild request to fill out the dining table in August, and my continued prayer routine with Janet, I was pregnant again. Janet was disappointed to hear this and addressed me –

"Gwen, I can't believe you were praying for yourself."

"Janet, I was praying for you! Let us keep praying for your gift, and God will bless you in due course."

******

Like clockwork, at eight weeks I saw the deep crimson

Jehovah Rapha – God Heals

spot in my underwear, an unbroken pattern resurfacing, just as I was trying to stitch the pieces of my life back together. In the past, I would have waited a few days before going to the doctor, making an appointment for the weekend; I didn't allow my personal life to interrupt the flow of work. This time I didn't wait.   I made the appointment immediately.

On a bright, sunny Thursday afternoon in December 2000, we rushed to the obstetrician. Dr. Black was the top obstetrician and gynecologist in my city and had delivered my two children. It was he who told me, three times, that I could try again after delivering the sad news of my miscarriages.

I sat and waited anxiously in the waiting room filled with expectant mothers; some were visible ready to deliver with large bellies looking like balloons ready to pop. It had been seven years since I last glowed with the expectancy of motherhood and it seemed as if seven years ago would be my last time.

The bright afternoon sun beating on the windows of the waiting room seemed to mock me while cheering on the other mothers. "Mrs. Kameka," the nurse announced, her voice relieving me from my thoughts.   Mark held my hands, hoping for the best as we went into the dark room to face the painful truth it held for us.

The room was tiny, no larger than 7 feet by 8 feet. Dark drapes covered the windows as if to conceal my pain and prevent it from spilling onto others. The small bed in the center of the room held my secret longings. The heart monitor and the ultrasound machine stood to its right. A metal chair with its worn, black leather upholstery sat to the left of the bed, intended for Mark to sit, but neglected in his decision to stand by my side. I wondered about the men who sat in the chair, were they happy to be daddies or was this just an obligation for them? The doctor's rolling stool at the foot of the bed was like the judgment seat.

The room smelled of mixed emotions that took me back to times when I heard heartbeats like horses stampeding through a forest, and other times when there was only the quiet of my own heart. I wanted to listen to those sounds, the sounds my baby's pulsating heart telling me, "Mommy I am alive." And I wanted the doctor to show me the little pea-shaped person. I wanted to hear, "Your baby is growing as expected."

The bed was made with fresh paper, and I climbed on and waited for the doctor. Dr. Black entered the room and greeted us –

"So, what are the Kamekas up to today?"

He wanted to make the atmosphere cheery, and I complied, I smiled a sad, silent smile. Joy was a currency I couldn't afford at this time.

Dr. Black squeezed cold, clear gel onto my growing belly before he rubbed the heart monitor all around my middle section, searching for the heartbeat. The silence was loud and overpowering. I couldn't look at Mark. I didn't want to see his pain, and I didn't want him to see mine.

Our pain filled the room, and the doctor kept silent. He continued his fruitless search and studied the tiny screen. He would have to share the truth, and eventually, he broke the silence –

"There is no fetal pole."

His voice was lifeless. I knew what those words meant; this was my fourth-time hearing 'there is no fetal pole.' This was the fourth-time loss invaded my life, a permanent resident I already knew.

Another baby I will not get to know. There would be no swollen belly ready to pop, there would be no packing of my bags, there would be no rushing to the hospital, there would be no breastfeeding, there would be no baby naming, there would be no more babies for us.

Dr. Black tried to give us hope, "You are young," he said, "you have plenty more years to try again."

Sure, we were young, but how many more times can my heart break? How many more times can I suffer this loss? I was silent; there was nothing left in me. What do you say to a doctor when he breaks your heart? Thank him for nothing or find a way to blame him. I chose silence.

On a bright, sunny Thursday afternoon in December 2000, Dr. Black told us to make an appointment to do a Dilation and Curettage (D&C) the following Monday. Then he would remove the fetus, our baby, from its home, from my womb.

We went home in silence. The sun never stopped

shining, the clouds didn't weep with us, people on the road never stopped to mourn our loss, life went on as usual. Even our bodies betrayed us, our hearts kept beating, and our feet kept moving, taking us to the car, and so we went home.

******

I sat on the sofa in our living room, and Mark kneeled on the floor before me. He placed his hand on my belly and bowed his head as if in prayer. He is not the praying type, except when he is teaching the children to say grace at meals and recite their bed-time prayers. We sat there in silence for fifteen, maybe twenty minutes then Mark slowly raised his head smiling –

"The baby is alive," he whispered.

"What are you trying to say? "Don't play with my mind."

"I felt a heartbeat; it felt like a little button pulsing beneath my finger, our baby is alive."

He spoke as one with ironclad proof, I almost believed him. I am not naïve and suspected that the poor soul was trying to make me happy, trying to fix a broken situation. How do you get Humpty Dumpty back together when the egg is all broken? Who can put a broken egg back together? Surely not my husband! I faintly responded,

"Are you sure? How can you be so certain?"

"I know what I felt. There is a heartbeat."

Mark's words brought a twinge of hope to my heart. I mustered a smile and plastered it on my lips, but it never reached my eyes. A broken heart doesn't have enough light to bring joy to the eyes.

We waited anxiously for Monday. Monday came too soon. Apprehensively, we went back to the doctor's office, but we had no plans to do a D&C. I was too exhausted with grief to fight Mark's unwillingness to accept the truth Dr. Black had delivered. Since he had already made up his mind that the baby was alive, we were going to the doctor for a prenatal checkup, not a D&C.

The doctor indulged Mark and checked for a heartbeat, and the stillness of the machine shattered my heart again. He scanned the ultrasound machine, and there was no fetal pole; the blank screen shone darkness on the hope that Mark had placed in my heart.

Mark was dead wrong. Dr. Black was right; he was the expert. Hadn't he delivered thousands of babies in our city? And wasn't he the head of the gynecology and obstetrician faculty of the public hospital? He was right. Mark was wrong.

Mark is not one to conjure up imaginations; he is a practical man. However, his truth was not aligned with Dr. Black's expertise and his machine's infallibility. I wanted clarity, so I pushed for more answers –

"Doc if there is no baby why is my belly growing?"

"My dear, your belly will continue to grow as the sac is still intact. You need a D&C to prevent infection and improve your chances of a viable pregnancy in the future."

Jehovah Rapha – God Heals

Dr. Black kept talking, but my ears stopped listening. His pronouncements kept playing in my mind like a broken record.

"There is no fetal pole."

"You are young; you can try again."

"You need a D&C."

"Infections-future-baby-young-fetal poles-D&C."

Nothing made sense, and everything sounded like gibberish.

I had to come to terms with reality; there was no baby inside of me. All I had was a sac with water, and it would continue to grow until we came to our senses and followed doctor's orders, until we decided to have the D&C. My womb was not a home. It had become a wasteland.

Mark was sure of himself and stood unwavering in his decision –

"We are not doing a D&C because I felt a heartbeat."

The doctor replied sardonically, but he was gentle with his sarcasm –

"Well you are the daddy, and if you say there is a heartbeat, there is a heartbeat."

He told us to come back in two weeks, so we did.

******

At 11 weeks I had gained more than twice the weight of my prior pregnancies. My belly had ballooned, and I looked about five months pregnant. I knew I should have listened to the doctor; I felt like a fake walking around with a growing belly of nothing. The nurse called my name, and

Jehovah Rapha – God Heals

once again I stepped into the dark room climbed onto the bed made with fresh paper.

Dr. Black pulled out the heart monitor from its cradle and started the routine. He knew what he knows, and Dr. Black was trying to please two desperate parents holding on to a pulse that a father felt once, holding on to an empty sac of fluid he knew must be extracted for my health. He rubbed the cold, clear gel onto my belly and then the monitor on the base of my belly.

The monitor came alive and pounded like the hooves of a few horses, not thousands, but there were horses, and we were silent. Dr. Black got up from his stool, perplexed. He couldn't believe what he was hearing. He quickly turned to the ultrasound machine and there on the screen was the most beautiful fetal pole I ever saw.

There was life inside of me! A living baby was growing in my womb! I could not fill out the dining table, but there would be five of us next summer. God heard Mark's silent prayer!

I was silent, overwhelmed with joy. There were no words to communicate what I felt in my heart.

The nurse gave us a two-week appointment, and this time we didn't just go to our doctor with hope we went with unmatched certainty; we were going to have a baby after seven years and three miscarriages.

Week 13. I climbed onto the bed and gazed on the monitor to look at the fetal pole. The doctor kept poking and pushing my belly. He put more cold gel on the wand;

Jehovah Rapha – God Heals

he rubbed my belly again and again.

We grew concerned…

"Doc is something wrong with the baby?"

We were so happy to hear the heartbeat on our last visit that we never considered the possibility of a disability. I had forgotten Dr. Black's words after the second miscarriage –

"Mrs. Kameka, your babies aborted themselves because they were severely deformed."

The doctor stopped all activities, placed his hands on his hips. I braced myself for another blow. The look on his face didn't register sorrow, but I had given up on facts and realities, I lived in moments and sound bites. He turned to us and asked –

"How many babies did I said you were having?"

There is a verse in the Bible that says, *"God will give you back the years the locusts have eaten."* Joel 2 verse 25. Did God restore what I had lost? Yes, Yes! I got back the years the locusts ate. Before I could answer, Dr. Black placed the wand on my belly and pointed to one baby then pointed out another.

"You are having two babies. Congratulations!"

Sorrow and joy have the same effect. I was speechless. Mark hugged me, and we cried tears of joy. Mark said as he watched Dr. Black pointing to the babies on the tiny screen, he got taller and his chest expanded. Dr. Black called his nurses and shared our miracle. The nurses were in awe; they sprinkled us with congratulations and advice.

Jehovah Rapha – God Heals

Laughter filled the room and spilled out into the streets, encouraging the sun to smile at us. Everyone looked like a friend, and I wanted to share the good news with strangers. My heart wouldn't stop laughing.

******

God had looked upon my family with kindness; He heard a father's silent prayer. The prayer of a broken man who lost three babies and was losing his wife, his marriage, and his family. The Bible is filled with stories of mothers who prayed to conceive, but in Mark 5 verse 42, a father sought Jesus in his desperation when his daughter fell ill and eventually died, and Jesus raised his daughter from the dead.

How can I believe in the miracles of the Bible, but not believe that God can restore a miscarriage and perform miracles in my life?

I believe! I believe!

Many will read this and say the doctor misdiagnosed my miscarriage, but I know this is a magnificent work of God. I know at eight weeks, not even the mother can feel the baby's movement in her womb, but God showed up and provided a pulse for my husband. How else but God?

The twins were born that following summer, weighing 6 ½ and 6 ¾ lbs. A natural birth, thirty-nine seconds apart. Today my girls are getting ready for college. They will forever be our gifts and our heartbeats.

I now see hope in every child, no matter how precarious their situation seems and my job and yours is to

Jehovah Rapha – God Heals

seek ways to help them to realize the greatness they possess.

I was recently thumbing through the Bible and came across Job 42 verse 10, *"After Job had prayed for his friends, the LORD restored his fortunes and gave him twice as much as he had before."* The passage reminded me of my difficulties getting pregnant and the mornings I prayed with Janet Robinson. It made me realize that when we turn our focus from ourselves, we can receive God's blessings twofold. By the way, Janet had her first child, in October 2001, four months after my twins were born.

******

God hears our prayers.
With God all things are possible.
Do not worship the pains of the past.
Do not focus on your pain; focus on the possibilities for
your friends.

Jehovah Rapha – God Heals

2

A 12 Year Mystery Solved

"And a woman was there who had been afflicted for twelve years by an issue of bleeding. She had suffered greatly under the care of many doctors and had spent all she had, but with no success. Instead, her condition had only grown worse." Mark 5 verses 25-26

Doctors ordered every blood work on the lab form, and I complied.

I got poked and prodded, repeatedly.

I did HIV/Aids tests, and they were negative.

I did liver and kidney checks, and they offered no clue.

I was x-rayed, dyed, and digitally imaged, and I got referred to a urologist.

I had two cystoscopies and a colonoscopy.

I did doppler ultrasounds; the results were inconclusive.

I had three miscarriages, and one baby was sent to the lab for testing.

Each test result brought relief but added another question mark. For 12 years I placed my trust in doctors, and for 12 years I suffered in the silent rage of an

Jehovah Rapha – God Heals

undiagnosed illness with no cure.

I've listened to doctors searching the minds of their more experienced colleagues about my situation, only to face me empty-handed. I've watched doctors pulling out large textbooks, pouring over diagnoses after diagnoses trying to find me a cure only to tell me that my case was extraordinary. Extraordinary? Who cares about extraordinary? I only wanted a cure and a name for what ailed me.

******

The intense discomfort on the left side of my abdomen started in 1994. It was not a pain, more like severe exhaustion radiating from my inside. A dull, dragging sensation. The only relief I got was from pressing hard on the area, and the relief was short-lived. I couldn't keep walking around with my hands stuck to my abdomen, so I relented and went to the doctor.

My husband and I spent several hours visiting General Practitioners, Urologists, and Gynecologists. I went to the best doctors in my city, Montego Bay, and when they could not find the problem, they sent me to the best doctors in the capital city, Kingston. I remember sitting across a young doctor in my community, Dr. Tannor, who, after getting the results of my blood work from the lab told me –

"Mrs. Kameka, your results are remarkable."

I had no clue what a doctor's remarkable meant and so I asked –

"Dr. Tannor what are you trying to tell me?"

"The lab work says nothing is wrong with you and I cannot find anything wrong with you."

He thought this was all in my head. The doctor was blaming the patient because he did not know how to cure me. I had the physical evidence to prove all wasn't well with my body.

I was chronically ill and undiagnosed for so long that guilt followed me like a wrecking ball. Guilt grew as I counted the number of hours Mark spent driving me to all these doctors. Guilt snowballed as I couldn't come to terms with the money we were spending on me, money we could've used for home repairs, buying things the children needed, or even buying a decent car. The guilty heart has one friend, loneliness, and loneliness extinguishes the fight to live.

******

What is the name of what I had? Was that too much to ask? I had already accepted my fate and had reached a point where I didn't care if the illness was terminal. All I wanted was the name of what was killing me.

My bladder would not empty and left me with an extremely unpleasant situation. Every trip to the bathroom painted the air with a persistent stench, the color of shame. No longer could I hide my illness, it exposed me. At work, I waited until the bathroom was empty and rushed to use it. If someone enters while I was there, I remained quiet and still in the cubicle until everyone left. I never wanted to be associated with the smell that my own body produced.

Jehovah Rapha – God Heals

How could this be? I was only 24 when this all started.

The urologist, Dr. Waterbury, performed a cystoscopy, I got brief relief. During the surgery, he removed a small tumor, the main cause of the blockage. Two years later, I had another cystoscopy and a colonoscopy; this time there was no relief. My situation worsened. I was desperate for a cure, so I lied, telling Mark the surgery was a success.

Each doctor's visit left me with more worries and less money. More shame and less love for life.

******

In the book of 1Peter chapter 5 verse 7, we are told, "Cast all your anxiety on Him, because He cares for you." Not some, but all. I could have saved myself 12 years of anxiety if only I had surrendered all to God instead of trying to work my way into God's heart with good works. The anxiety of which I speak is not so much a cure for my illness but the worry that weighed me down during that time. Not all illnesses will be cured on this side of life. We can be ill and still have joy if we cast our cares on God.

I tried to find my own joy - I busied myself with activities: I did more than everyone, I worked longer hours than most, I took on back-breaking projects, and I pushed myself to the limit. I got the admiration of friends, my extended family basked in my achievements, and colleagues at work sought my expertise.

Everyone saw a strong, fearless woman who could break down any barrier in her way and they rewarded me with praises and accolades. But when the day settled, and I

Jehovah Rapha – God Heals

had those quiet moments by myself, the emptiness of my life overwhelmed me.   And neither the praises nor the rewards were enough to penetrate the emptiness that engulfed me.   Sometimes the strongest friend is the weakest, the happiest one is the saddest, and the one who is the life of the party is the loneliest.

******

Eventually, I told Mama that I wasn't well, and she told me to read God's words back to Him and asked for healing.   I couldn't; it seemed sacrilegious. It wasn't sacrilegious, I was in bondage with fear, pride, guilt, and shame, and didn't have a relationship with God.

Total surrender would change me…total surrender to God.   A life surrendered is a life of complete freedom, wrapped in the everlasting love of God. Surrender brings the joy that radiates throughout the heart as bright as the sun.   Surrender doesn't mean trouble won't come your way; it means you won't carry the weight of your troubles.

******

August 2004, this was the chance I have been waiting on for ten years.   My new job in the USA would give me the opportunity to see the best doctors in the world and reclaim my life. My excitement didn't last long. The new doctors offered nothing new. I repeated the cycle for two more years; I got poked, prodded, x-rayed, and imaged with no answer.

The transition to the USA was a drastic change for my family; we didn't have the support of our siblings, parents, or close friends. Overnight trips from my parents were no more, weekend drives to the country to visit Mark's mother were in the past, and Sunday evening dinners with my sister-in-law and her children were just cherished memories. Gone too was our financial stability. Mark couldn't find work for a year. Even my impeccable professional career was blown over like a house made of straw. I had to prove myself all over again to people who seem to resent my presence. The accolades and rewards dissipated, and the external noise quieted.

Without a doubt, I knew that God took me to the USA to kill me: I was sicker, poorer, and lonelier in a place I knew He had sent me. I was surely going to die. I eventually did, but not the physical death that I had anticipated.

******

In the USA, I was sequestered from the people and things that fostered my self-sufficiency, fed my pride, and poisoned my soul. God brought me to the USA and gave me a second chance to live my life with joy, to renew me, and to redeem me. First, I had to die to self...I have now learned that a seed must die before it can bear fruit. I have also learned that our troubles are not here to ruin us but to refine us. God didn't will my illness on me, but he would use the experience to make me whole.

For the first time in my life, I was forced to turn inward. It was in my quietness that I actively pursued a relationship with God. Not a rushed prayer in the morning

Jehovah Rapha – God Heals

kind of relationship, to check the prayer box. Neither the harried prayer to fill an urgent need. It is the kind of relationship you have with a close friend, the one who knows all your secrets and you know theirs.

God became my confidant and friend. I talked with God about my every thoughts and desires – I looked to God for His knowledge to navigate Corporate America, I asked for wisdom in dealing with new challenges at work. I turned to God for every decision, large and small, even guidance on what I should wear to work.

What happens when you talk to someone daily and share your inner thoughts with him? The person gets to know you, the person reveals himself to you, you develop mutual trust, you may even fall in love, soon, you will be saying 'my friend.' I fell in love with God and I accepted His love that was already waiting for me. I became a friend of God. I found a church and took the ultimate step. On February 13, 2005, I was baptized by water immersion, a public acknowledgment of my love for the Divine. Did you know that God wants to be your friend? Yes, God wants to be your friend and wants to draw you close to Him.

I began to search the Bible and got to know the heart and mind of God. I learned that God's love for us is unchanging – there is nothing that we could ever do that could make the Divine not love us. God's love for us is radical. His love radiates all over the pages of the Bible:

Jehovah Rapha – God Heals

- God forgave David after he committed adultery and murder.
- I read how God took the Israelites from a life of slavery in Egypt through the difficult path of the Red Sea to a land flowing with goodness.
- He promoted Joseph out of prison to be second in command over Egypt.
- I saw on the pages of the Bible that Jesus protected the prostitute and the women who cheated on their husbands and gave them the gift of compassion.
- And the ultimate gift, Christ gave his life to redeem me even though He saw all my sins. Not some, all the evil things I had done, from defacing my mother's bed after she disciplined me when I was four years old to neglecting my marriage.

"God proved His love for us in this: While we were still sinners Christ gave His life for us." Romans 5 verse 8.

******

I came to the USA for health and wealth only to find unmatched treasure – a relationship with the Divine, the Creator of everything that I was seeking. It is like sitting at Maya Angelou's feet and receiving her counsel instead of reading her books, but this was exponentially greater. I surrendered and received the abundant life, a life dependent on the Divine, a life filled with joy.

God used my first two years in the USA to transform a strong-willed woman who had enjoyed doing things her way. He was molding me into one who not only looked great on the outside but was beautiful on the inside too. God transformed me and filled me up with His love, His grace, and His joy.

We have two choices: Self-will that leads to suffering or Surrender that leads to satisfaction in the Divine.

Suffering was a small parenthesis in my transformation. Throughout your lifetime you will see these pauses: financial loss, illness, death, jail, and friends and family members who will despise you and even try to harm you. Whatever troubles you face do not fear them, surrender your will to God. The Divine will take you to the other side of your troubles where joy and peace reside.

2 Corinthians 12 verse 9, the apostle Paul wrote, *"And he said unto me, My grace is sufficient for thee: for my strength is made perfect in weakness."* He went on to say in verse 10, *"For when I am weak, I am strong."*

******

In surrender, I became weak and gave up on self-sufficiency and I ran to Jesus for help and I prayed –

"Heavenly Father you are holy, and I thank you for your love. Fill me with your presence. Never leave me nor forsake me. Father, you promised to take care of me as I entered this new land, so God I am relying on you for my every need. Teach me your ways and impart your wisdom and knowledge in me. Thank you for your love. Thank you for what you have done that I am yet to see. Amen."

Jehovah Rapha – God Heals

No longer strong on my own, I surrendered my entire life to God. I read His words back to Him. Exodus 15:26 "The Lord Who Heals" – *"I am Jehovah who heals you both in body and soul. In body, by preserving from and curing diseases, and in soul, by pardoning iniquities."*

12 years after my first doctor's visit,

12 years of suffering,

All this would end…where God is, all is well.

******

I woke up in the hospital as they were taking me out of the operating room. There was nothing special about this hospital: plain white walls, long corridors, dim lights, and a nurses' station. I was laying on a rolling bed, wearing a white surgery gown, and my head was covered with a white cotton fabric folded in a triangle.

Everything looked blurry. I blinked a few times before I could see clearly. As I looked around, trying to grasp hold of something or someone familiar, I noticed a young man in a doctor's coat at the foot of my bed. He talked with the nurse at the nurses' station while he handed her some papers in a blue envelope with my name on it. His face wasn't visible, but I could see the nape of his neck. He had a deep olive complexion. His short, brown hair was partially covered with a blue cotton cap. Even with his coat on, I could see that he was a skinny man, no more than 160 pounds. There was another person standing beside me, a replica of the young doctor. Both men had an air of familiarity about them. I tilted my head to the left and

Jehovah Rapha – God Heals

faced the young man at my bedside and asked –

"What happened to me?"

He replied –

"You just had surgery and the doctor is closing your files."

He pointed to the doctor talking with the nurse –

"See that man talking with the nurse; he is your surgeon."

"What surgery?"

"Catheterization and Ca...erization."

He spoke quickly and in a whispered tone. All these words were new to me, but I was too disoriented to ask for clarification. As the anesthetic wore off and I gathered my senses, I realized that though the men seem familiar I had never met them before and I cannot recall checking into a hospital.

I sat up. As I looked around I realized that I was no longer in the hospital, I was in my own bed. The dream seemed real, and the details of my memory were vivid. I looked across the room saw Mark sitting at the computer. I jumped off the bed and sat beside him and related the entire dream. I asked him to look for the word. Since I never heard the word before I thought it was one word and the same surgery done twice. It took us some time to find out that these were two different words and two separate processes.

Catheterization - a process to empty the bladder

Cauterization - a process to burn and heal.

Jehovah Rapha – God Heals

On a cold wintry Sunday morning in February 2006, a mysterious doctor performed my surgeries at Marathon Terrace in Maryland. After 12 years of not knowing and suffering, I got the treatment that I needed. Exhausted and dazed from the reality of what took place I spent most of the day in bed. I used the bathroom, sniffed the air and there was nothing to smell. My urine no longer had that thick, greasy look, and there was no odor. I am healed; I am healed. I repeated those words quietly to myself and then to Mark –

"I am healed, I am healed."

Like the woman with the issue of blood I got my healing when I reached out and touched Jesus – *"Daughter,"* said Jesus, *"your faith has healed you. Go in peace and be free of your affliction."* Mark 5 verses 33-34.

Earlier I shared with you – not all illnesses will be cured on this side of heaven and some we must get a doctor's treatment. December 31, 2014, at 12:35 in the afternoon I received the dreaded news –

"Mrs. Kameka, I am sorry to tell you…you have medullary thyroid carcinoma."

I had surgery and two challenging years that followed. Only this time, cancer found me surrendered to God and rooted in my faith. I was no longer on my own; I had the warm hand of God to carry me through the tough times.

Jehovah Rapha – God Heals

Where do you turn when your money cannot save you? To whom do you look when men fail you? We must turn to Jehovah Rapha, the Healer.

******

Surrender All.
Become a friend of God.
Come to God just as you are.
Complete joy comes only from God.

3

Prescription from Heaven

"Now it happened after these things that the son of the woman who owned the house became sick. And his sickness was so serious that there was no breath left in him." 1 King 17 verse 17.

"Take him home and make him comfortable. There is nothing that we can do to save him." The young doctor casually pronounced my brother dead without saying the word. The euphemistic 'make him comfortable' translated clearly to my parents. With no money for private doctors to get a second opinion, Mama and Dada took Warren home in the dark of the night.

******

Warren was a special child. It is the kind of specialness that came packaged with the delicate breathe of uncertainty and the full force of hope. His birth was brutally unusual for my family and was rather difficult. It started under the full glare of nosey neighbors hungry for gossip and was completed in a hospital in the remote city of Falmouth Trelawny, among strangers. Thirty-five miles from the energetic but humble community in Mount Salem,

Jehovah Rapha – God Heals

Piggott Street, the place we called home. The place where children cracked nuts with large stones under the shade of the almond trees, where we played skip and rounders, where boys made cars from discarded juice boxes, where neighbors played their music too loud, the place where everyone knows everybody's business and neighbors cared for each other.

1979 was a tumultuous year for Jamaica, our politics had soured and had spilled over in the lives of ordinary people. It was a time of deep turbulence, violence, and extreme hardships. Several hundred Jamaicans were brutally murdered for wearing the wrong color, any color affiliated to a political party. School children were included in the casualties just for wearing their uniforms. Aid from the USA evaporated leaving most of the people without social services. Tourists were advised not to travel to our country, businesses closed, unemployment skyrocketed, food was scarce, and medical care was substandard, nearly non-existent. The fragility of our lives was exposed, and this was the cradle in which my brother Warren was born.

******

It was a sunny afternoon, September 14, 1979, and Mama was ready to deliver her eighth child. We had a problem, the hospital in our town was shut down due to a fire and lack of funds to make the repairs. My brother Donald ran and got the midwife, Nurse Clarke. Nurse Clarke came as quickly as she was called, dressed in white and carried a large black bag. The scene was curious - nosey neighbors piled up in the lane, pressed up against the barbed wire fence, they strained their ears to listen to the sounds of birthing. I stood by the gate to chase them away encouraged by the shock of the spectacle. I gave them a look. The look that Mama said makes people feel small. I can do as I please now, Mama is busy, she cannot see me, and she cannot tell me to respect my elders. The look quickly cleared the lane and the women walked away with their children in tow, hissing their teeth at me.

The nurse worked feverishly, but the baby got lodged in the birth canal and made home delivery impossible. Someone, I can't remember who, got a taxi to take Mama and Nurse Clarke to the nearest hospital in Falmouth, Thirty-five miles away.

The shadow of death hung over our home; there was no guarantee that Mama would make it to the hospital on time or if they would make it back home to us. I was nine years old, but I understood the dangers facing Mama and the baby.

My siblings and I, plus a few children from the neighborhood ran behind the car. Hot, salty tears obscured my vision, love for Mama carried my tiny legs as I ran down the dusty, rocky lane, up the potholed filled road, until the car disappeared.

Before Nurse Clarke left with Mama, I overheard her telling Dada in a hushed voice –

"Mr. Bell, I will do everything to take care of your

wife, but this is a serious situation."

In my mind this meant death.

Dada got dressed and left for Falmouth. He returned late in the night and delivered the good news; Mama and the baby were ok.

Everyone thought Warren's birth was a miracle and as a gift of celebration, he was chosen to be baby Jesus in the annual Christmas play at our church.

******

1980 came and with it, the political violence escalated. The winds of poverty and hardships covered the vulnerable poor across the entire island. Murder rates hiked, acts of violence were more heinous than before, the economy tanked further, and we suffered like no other time. Shelves in the grocery stores stood bare; Shopkeepers hid supplies beneath counters or in back rooms and sold the things we wanted such as flour, sugar, milk, rice, and chicken to their friends and 'important' people. Pipes in the poorer neighborhoods were dry, and our only salvation for a drop of drinking water was the government trucks. There were days when the water truck didn't show up and we had no choice but to go to the nearby, wealthy communities to fill containers using their garden hose. We walked four miles to the river to wash our clothes.

Our trips to the river were fun. The boys jumped from the cliff to the deep end of the river, making perfect splashes. They skipped stones across the water, each one trying to out-do the previous performance. I was amazed at all the skills the boys possessed. I tried skipping rocks but failed. We had tons of fun learning to swim and wading in the water after pieces of clothing as they slipped from our mothers' wash tubs.

The women chatted while they scrubbed dirty clothes and the older girls helped their mothers with the washing. The smaller girls, like me, helped to hang the clothes on the bushes to dry.

The river was filled with crayfish, mullets, and jangas hiding beneath slippery stones. The men catch them using straw baskets. Later in the day, the men prepared lunch of boiled bananas and steamed fish which we ate from banana leaves. In those moments we forgot the hardships of our community.

After lunch, we searched for the sun and moved the clothes to the spot where it had rested. Late in the afternoon, the men cut sugar cane and we relaxed in the shade of the bamboo trees chewing on the sweet stick and drinking the sweet syrupy juice, some escaping our lips, running down our arms and legs which were now ashen from overexposure to the river water. As the sun escaped to the west of the island and the cool breeze chilled the river, we folded our clothes and packed the wash tubs. The men carried the wash tubs on their heads. We skipped and laughed as we returned to our homes with the light breeze brushing against our skin. The darkness of the evening covered our faces.

The realities of the hardships faced us when we

Jehovah Rapha – God Heals

returned home.

Doctors and nurses were laid off from the public hospitals and the hospitals were littered with the sick waiting for care. During the crisis, our family needed the hospital and once again it failed us. Warren was facing danger one more time.

******

He was seven months old and teething. Sometimes, teething babies drooled like a puppy on a hot summer's day and so it was with Warren. We were changing his bibs and shirts around the clock as his newly formed teeth pushed against his gum. We were happy when the drooling stopped. Our happiness was short-lived when we noticed his belly ballooning, and he cried incessantly. His cries turned into deep non-stop wails. He had no bowel movements and stopped peeing. Warren was baby number eight, and my parents had never experienced anything like this with the other seven children.

My parents took no chances with home remedies and took him to the hospital. By this time his eyes were sunken, the wailing had stopped, he did not have the strength to cry. Warren whimpered like a puppy left out in the rain. My brother looked like a child with kwashiorkor, lacking the orange hair. He looked exactly like the little children you see in advertisements raising funds for malnourished children around the world. The doctor took his vitals, looked at my parents, and told them –

"Take the child home and make him comfortable."

Jehovah Rapha – God Heals

"There is nothing we can do to save him."

Make him comfortable? Isn't he the miracle baby? Didn't God save him at birth?

Dada was angry. He said the doctor only gave up because he looked at him and Mama and judged them for being poor. He thought the doctor gave up because there was no need for another poor child from the ghetto to survive. My father cursed the doctor and Mama prayed.

Sometimes the only thing a poor man has to show how much he cares for his family is his rage. A man who cannot protect his children or provide for them is like a wounded lion with enough energy to make one more attack. I see these wounded lions walking the streets of the ghetto daily.

My mother refused to accept the finality of the doctor's diagnosis. Mama was never one to give up. She had already experienced the mighty hand of God in her life. I was there when she asked God for a house and God provided a home. Mama knew God and the power of God. She took her baby home and presented the dying child to the Healer, Jehovah Rapha.

"God will create a way," Mama said.

******

There was an old lady in the community who was as old as time, Nana Bee. She was the tiniest and oldest adult I had ever met. She stood no more than four feet tall with skin that looked like aged leather stretched loosely across her bony frame. Intricate lines carefully etched across her

Jehovah Rapha – God Heals

forehead deepens when she scolded the children in her care. Her head was always tied, and she wore long sleeved dresses with frills that hung below her knees.

Nana Bee was the community's nanny and herbalist. She knew all the herbs and their healing properties and had bottles of potions made from various herbs lining the shabby shelves above her dining table and on the floor of her one bedroom. She spent all day boiling and straining roots, leaves, and plants to rid us of colds, tummy aches, itches, and all ailments.

I knew her well; she cared for me and my brother Mark when I was three years old. Every morning after Mama dropped us off at Nana Bee's home; Nana Bee gave me a mixture of blended Aloe Vera and Leaf-of-Life juices. I hurriedly swallowed the green, slimy concoction to get the reward, a spoonful of sugar. Nana Bee was strict and set in her ways, and at age three I had a lot to teach her, but she wouldn't learn. She saw me as rebellious. I was the first and only child to be dismissed from her care. After six months with Nana Bee, she had enough of me. One evening she said no more.

"Miss Gloria, me can't tek care a yu likkle girl no more she too womanish."

My mother pleaded with Nana Bee,

"It can't be too bad. Wha she do?"

Nana Bee was bent over the wood fire stirring a pot of putrid smelling leaves. She didn't stop her stirring to have the discussion.

Jehovah Rapha – God Heals

"Likkle gal scornful. Every time me feed har bredda she wash de bokkle."

"Michelle, yu promise not to wash yu bredda bottle."

 "But de bottle black Mama."

"Yu see it. Likkle woman. No manners, no respect. Can't tek care of har."

All I did was to wash the soot from the wood stove that Nana Bee used for cooking and boiling her medicines from my brother's bottle.

"Try sen har to school."

"But Nana Bee, she too young."

"No, if she can wash bokkle she can go a school."

Nana Bee got the last word and the next day, at three years old I was in pre-elementary school. I believed that her green potion is the reason I never get the flu. Nana Bee died a few years after she gave me an early start to education. Who could Mama turn to for help?

******

Mama prayed and wept before God. The embers of light from the kerosene lamp cast her shadow on the thin, floral curtain that separated my parent's bedroom from where we (children) slept. She was on her knees, her head bowed. Sleep closed my eyelids and took the worry with it. I guess Mama went to sleep eventually because the next morning she told us she had a dream, and she got a prescription from heaven.

In her dream, Mama saw Nana Bee. Nana Bee gave Mama detailed instructions:

Jehovah Rapha – God Heals

"Mek Marvia (my eldest sister) pick four naseberry leaves before de morning dew disappear. No bodda wash de leave dem or yu dego wash off de medicine fi heal de likkle bwoy."

"Marvia fi put one cup a wata inna de pot and den put de leaves dem inna de wata. Boil de wata until e reach bout half a cup."

"Mek e cool. No mek e get cold doh. Likkle warmish. No put no suga in deh. Den mek de bwoy drink every drop."

Mama said she couldn't wait for the sun to rise, her child was lying beside her taking short, shallow breaths that seemed like his last.

Mama got up early in the morning, told us (all her children) the dream and followed the instructions as she received them. Within the hour after emptying the cup, my brother had bowel movements, and before the day ended the dying child sat up, moved around, and he drooled as if it had never stopped.

******

"But there is a spirit in a man, the breath of the Almighty, that gives him understanding." Job 32:8

Jehovah Rapha – God Heals

God, the Almighty resides in all of us, and He will reveal the secrets of this world to us when we make ourselves available to listen and to learn. When you call on Jesus all things are possible. When the doctors give up on you our God the Great Healer, Jehovah Rapha is working on your miracle.

******

God uses nature to serve us.
God shows himself to us in ways that we can understand.
God resides within us and will reveal the secrets of this world when we make ourselves available.
Greater is the God that is in you than all the wise men in the world.

Jehovah Rapha – God Heals

God Almighty
El-Shaddai

Almighty God -- Our all-sufficient supply -- Bestower of power – gifts – blessings -- and the one who makes us fruitful.

4

The Sun Will Rise After the Rain

"But as for you, you meant evil against me; but God meant it for good, in order to bring it about as it is this day, to save many people alive." Genesis 50:20.

As a little girl, I enjoyed playing in the rain. I recalled the rainy day when my eldest brother, Toney, packed us two by two on Mama's bedside rug; the one intricately woven with four cute kittens with golden thread forming their piercing eyes. Toney pulled us down the steps leading from our two-bedroom apartment as we squealed and shouted with delight, stripped down to our underwear.

October 26, 1987, I am not the little girl gliding down the steps in the rain, laughing with pleasure. I am a 17-year-old college student standing in the rain because I had no place to go. I am 120 miles away from home with the cold evening rain gently beating down on me. Each rounded drop of rain was slowly washing away my dreams as I had planned them.

I had no place to shelter from the rain, and worse, I had no place to sleep. Our well-thought-out plan for my boarding while I had attended college was quickly falling

El-Shaddai – God Almighty

apart.

Returning home to Montego Bay was not an option I could entertain. I refused to give up on college and had made up my mind to sleep beneath the stars if that is what it will take to earn a college degree. I rested on the promises of the future to erase the pain of my present situation.

******

College? This cannot be real. Michelle Gwendolyn Bell is going to college. I hugged myself tightly and twirled before the mirror. I wanted to shout, but I was too afraid that I might wake myself up from this dream. I was giddy from disbelief, and my head pounded from the excitement. Next month will be the start of new things for my family and me. I was the only child of nine children to attend high school, and now I was heading to college. College was going to change our lives, a ticket out of poverty.

Just nine years before, my neighbor Jerry scornfully laughed in my face when I told him I wanted to attend Mt. Alvernia High school. Jerry wasn't just my neighbor he was my good friend, and I had to share with him the secret, my dreams, a desire I was soon to find out from him was too lofty for a girl wearing threadbare hand-me-down clothes.

I climbed over the barbed wire fence that separated our yards and searched for my friend; when I found him, Jerry was sitting idly on the steps that led to his house,

El-Shaddai – God Almighty

and was shaving a piece of wood with a pen knife.

"Jerry, Jerry I am going to tell you something, but you must promise not to tell anybody."

Jerry nodded in agreement.

"Jerry, I am going to go to Mt. Alvernia High."

Mt. Alvernia High was the most prestigious high school for girls in my city and seems that the 100 or so spaces available for 11-year-old girls were reserved for girls from middle-income families who attended private prep schools.   Only the brightest who earned excellent grades in the government exams could get in. I had two more years before I could sit the exams, but I dreamed incessantly about the crisp, white uniform and the precise blue tie.

An unbelievable sense of purpose washed over me, just from imagining my name in the national newspaper with Mt. Alvernia imprinted beside it. I know I would look cute in the white uniform and blue tie. It was too much not to share outside the walls of my home, someone other than Mama had to know my dreams and someone other than my mother needs to be happy for me. I also wanted my friend to look at my family with some esteem. I have now learned that some friendships can only be maintained if you keep a ranking one step lower than the perceived friend. I didn't know that not all associations should not be placed in the friend category; I was only eight years old.

The instant the words slipped from my tongue I wished I could have shaken Jerry's ears, retrieved them, and

El-Shaddai – God Almighty

salvaged my dignity. To my horror, Jerry laughed at me,
the kind of laugh that got him bent over and slapped his
own knees. When he recovered from knocking over my
dreams, he went in for the kill, slathering words like salt in
the fresh wounds he had created.

"You can't even afford de soap fi wash white
uniform bout yu waan fi go a Mt. Alvernia."

Jerry's words crushed me.   My eight-year-old me
wasn't so sure Mt. Alvernia High was attainable anymore.
Jerry was probably right; we were so poor if it weren't for
his family's kindness we would not have bread at times. If
it weren't for his mother's generosity, we wouldn't watch
Dallas, Bonanza, and Lands of the Giant.

Miss Mary, Jerry's mother, allowed us to lie on our
bellies on the verandah with strict commands that our feet
did not touch the floor to soil it. We made ourselves small,
feet in the air and watched the 30-inch screen 20 feet away.
We had a television but couldn't pay for electricity, so it sat
on top of the buffet with its cherished plates and cups that
were never used unless we had visitors.

Jerry's words assaulted my dreams and I walked one
step closer to the box he wanted to put me in, 'the poor girl
who will always be poor.' I looked down at my feet, where
my dreams fell, I picked them up, dusted them off, and
dragged them behind me as I walked away. When I told
Mama what Jerry said to me, Mama gave me firm comfort
– "Me dawta, no mek nobady stop yu from dreaming.
Continue fi dream big. An yu see when dem laff afta

El-Shaddai – God Almighty

yu it mean sey yu on de right path. If dem no laff afta yu, yu not dreaming big enuff."

Mama wasn't educated, but she was wise. I hid Mama's words in my heart, and I used her words to erase Jerry's terrible scorn. Mama's words carried me throughout the years like a super shield protecting me from pejoratives meant to disarm my ambition; words meant to keep me in my place. Words like: 'you cannot accomplish this,' 'you are not good enough,' 'it is impossible,' or 'you do not belong here.'

******

I never knew anyone from my community who had gone to college, finishing high school was the epitome of success where I lived. On the evening of my high school graduation in July 1986, after I received my diploma, the ghosts of all the unlived dreams, dreams belonging to children whose college ambitions were diverted to the workforce too early, haunted me. Their reality was now mine. I wept bitterly, weeping until my body ached and I gasped for breath. I saw the same deep sorrow in my classmates who were facing the same ghosts.

Children in the ghetto are commodities, and each child must pay the price for their existence, some with their bodies, others give their lives. The teenage mothers you see are not bad girls, these are girls who went in search for food, bus fare, money to buy books, and they got caught up in the vicious cycle of poverty, another baby too soon, another mouth that will not be fed. So many young boys

El-Shaddai – God Almighty

didn't outlive their teenage years. They went hustling to help pay the bills and the powerful net of the gang snatched them, eventually, taking their lives. Ghetto children are massively neglected by loving mothers who must get to work before the sun rises and return home by the light of the moon.

The educated child from a low-income family carries a heavy burden; the hopes and dreams of everyone in their community are hitched onto theirs. The moment a flicker of hope is seen in a child, the child signs a blank check for every family member. Too often, family members cash their checks too soon and for too much.

After graduating High School, I interviewed for an Accounts Payables Clerk position at the Seasons Hotel, and at the same time, I applied for placement in the Community College. I was successful in both endeavors.

"Mama I got a job at Seasons Hotel as an Accounts Payables Clerk."

"But yu did tell me say yu get inna de community college too."

"Yes, Mama."

"What Payables Clerk do?"

"Pay people who work for the hotel and people who supply goods to the hotel, and file paperwork."

"Soh tell me what de boss do?"

"Not too sure Mama, but I guess the boss oversees everything."

"Well, yu can be de boss enuh." If yu go a college, yu

can come back and oversee everything."

"But Mama..."

"No buts." "I will find a way, and God will provide." "Yu tink me wash people clothes and clean people house fi yu go file paper? Yu can do betta dan dat." "Yu going to college." "Me proud a yu."

Mama was her wise self again; she took the burden of early adult life from my shoulders and gave me a shot at being the 'boss.' Mama didn't cash her check. How could she be that brave? Taking on college expenses and giving up the income that I could be taking home to help, money that the family badly needed. She knew how much I dreamed of going to college. For years she had listened to my college and career plans, and for years she has been praying how to handle this day.

******

Going to college was a massive achievement for my family. My going to college is as big an event for my family as landing on the moon was to the USA. Dada dropped out of school to earn a living before he was 12 years old and Mama when she was 14 years old.

Look at what God has done. I am on my way to Kingston - on my way to the College of Arts Science and Technology - on my way to CAST.

August 1987, I went to College on a wing and a prayer, all bundled up in faith and hope, and the promises of God. Mama always believed that when you trust in God with all your heart that God will protect, provide, and deliver you.

El-Shaddai – God Almighty

I had no books; I barely had any clothes, I had my bus fare for the first month and the warmth of a promise from Auntie C that I had a place to sleep. That promise was short-lived and turned out to be a mockery or a stepping stone, depending on how you view my story. I view that promise as a doorway that was opened by God.

******

On a rainy Monday evening, October 26, 1987, after only six weeks in college, Auntie C told me I had to move out immediately. She didn't even allow me to collect my clothes. I was standing right there before her, just inches from her face, yet she threw my clothes in the dirt. She stood like a bulwark in the doorway as if to block my view from seeing the bed and denying me the pleasure of one last look of what I would not enjoy – a good night's sleep.

I tried to plea for my future –

"Auntie, wha me do, wha me do yu?

My pleas were useless. Auntie C shouted at me; she was filled with anger, her high-pitched voice hitting me, weakening my position.

"Leave, just leave, you cannot stay here. Not even one more night."

Could I not even spend the night? She muffled something about my uncle; I couldn't hear the words. I wondered what part my uncle played in all of this. My uncle was working overseas and agreed with my moving into the house.

It felt like someone punched me in the gut, pulled the

El-Shaddai – God Almighty

rug from beneath my 17-year-old feet. Imagine looking up in the sky all your life, gazing and wondering what was beyond the clouds and then you get a telescope. With that telescope, you could see the splendid stars, the unprecedented details of the galaxies, and the beauty of the planets. Without warning, the telescope is snatched from you and not only snatched, but your eyes are plucked out. Suffering from a loss is deepened when you have tasted the sweetness of the thing now lost.

I cannot finish college without my aunt's free boarding; this would be impossible. Mama is a domestic helper, and Dada is a bartender in the hotel. Dada only worked at the peak of the tourist season, November to May every year. During the offseason, he sold grocery items from a stall in the yard but could not earn enough to take care of nine children. The future of my family was tied to my success, and my success was inextricably intertwined with Auntie C's kindness. All five years of high school and one year in community college would be wasted, washed away in the rain at Mannings Hill Road and my family would be doomed if I accepted Auntie C's rejection and so I turned my back at the thought of returning home.

How could I finish college if I had no place to sleep? I begged my aunt for more than two hours to let me stay. I asked her for an explanation. If I knew what I did then I could fix my mistakes. She offered no answers. Sometimes whatever stirs a person to hate, maim or kill, and mistreat others come from within themselves. There is no salve you

El-Shaddai – God Almighty

and I could apply to their souls to redeem them except they take a good look in the mirror and seek their own redemption.

She slammed the door in my face. I sat in the remnants of her wrath and my heart burned with crimson red rejection. I, alone, sat on her red and white patio chair and wept silently; tears for myself, tears for my parents, and tears for my future self who would not achieve her goals.

With the slamming of a door, my aunt took away my telescope, but I still had my eyes because I still had my faith. I was determined, I must finish college even if I had to sleep on her patio chair for two more years. I cannot go back to Montego Bay. There was nothing there for me. Nothing.

******

Auntie C and I had a good relationship for 11 years. I met her when I was six years old when my mother's brother, uncle Stenford, introduced her to Mama as his wife. She was beautiful and well dressed. I thought she was a wealthy movie star; she reminded me of Lena Horne and Nancy Wilson. I fussed over her, bringing her glasses of water and running behind her wherever she went. She was always thrilled with my attention. I danced for her, and she belted out boisterous fits of laughs. At times calling my uncle's attention to my gyrations – "Stenford watch Michelle." Most times she handed me a dollar note for my dancing.

El-Shaddai – God Almighty

Just two Sundays ago we went to church together.
When we got home, I made her favorite pot-roast pork, and
she cooked rice and peas, and steamed cabbage. Later in
the evening, we took the bus to the National Heroes Park.
She even paid for a photographer to take a picture of me. I
was wearing a black and red checkered shirt with black
pants. Auntie C was going to share the picture with my
uncle the next time she writes to him.

******

Now ten days later, after the short holiday break, I
came back to my aunt, and she could not recognize me. I
was an unwelcome stranger in her eyes. Even if I was a
stranger, didn't she know that by helping the poor, she was
welcoming the presence of Christ in her home and she
would be blessed?

I read it in Matthew 25 verse 34. Jesus told the people
who gathered to hear Him speak, "*the King will say to the
people who helped the poor: Come, you who are blessed by
my Father; take your inheritance prepared for you since
the creation of the world.*"

God has an inheritance for all of us; giving to the poor
is one of the keys to activate your abundance.

Mama and Dada were always putting up strangers:
men, women, and children. We only had three bedrooms
for nine children and my parents, yet we always find a
place for another person to sleep. We always have a place
for a relative who left the country seeking a better life. Was
this God's repayment to my parents for their charitable

El-Shaddai – God Almighty

deeds?   God sees the ending when He created the beginning, and He had a check for my parents, one they will never outspend.   The Bible tells us, in Matthew 24 verse 35, *"Heaven and earth will pass away before any of His words pass away."* These words Christ spoke after His promise to those who will reap an inheritance for helping the poor.

******

I flipped through the pages of my mind to recall all our interactions; I searched for the moment that created this situation but could find none. I was far from perfect and was a challenging child – I had a mouth on me. I told people what I thought about them without filtering my words. Mama said that the way I looked at people could make them feel small in my presence. Mama warned me all the time to watch my attitude. I raked through my mind and could find nothing. I relied on my aunt to tell me, but she too came up empty.

God was changing me and preparing to expose me to a better life, but there I was trying to secure a spot in my aunt's heart and a place in her home. I had more needs than a place to sleep, needs I couldn't measure. I could not have predicted that I needed more than an education to work in an office. How could I have known that I would be working for fortune 500 companies and Multilateral Development Banks? I needed life skills and exposure to new lifestyles that my aunt could not afford to give me.

Why do we get anxious and upset when we face closed

El-Shaddai – God Almighty

doors? Remember, God has a plan for your life and it is better than the one you have planned for yourself.

God is constantly working in our favor if only we could see Him putting the pieces of our lives together for our good and His glory. We must stand in faith. Without faith, we will lean on our own understanding. Without faith, we will create the god of our liking to give us the things we want and that is where we miss our miracles.

******

I got a glimpse of a life outside the gates of poverty when I went to work with Mama in 1977. Mama worked in a beautiful home where children went to school every day, there was no lack of food, there was water in the pipes, and light bulbs glowed when the switches were flipped. They read newspapers, they sat around the dinner table and ate together, and they discussed future and current events. I wanted more of what I felt than what I saw, there was harmony between each family member, and I thought money and education filled their home with civility and calm.

My image of who I could be and what the world had to offer was eclipsed by my visit to that home. I left transformed and started to build castles in my mind. That was the day that planted the seed of Mt. Alvernia in my consciousness. I was seven years old. It is never too early to help children to dream of who they will become. Building castles meant arduous work, and I attacked my school work with vigor even at that early age. I approached

El-Shaddai – God Almighty

every day as if I was already living in a beautiful home.

If I am going to live the life I dreamed of and not the one handed to me I cannot leave Kingston. I concocted a plan to sleep on the patio chair until my aunt changed her mind and welcomed me back in her life and her apartment.

******

I have had deep intimate relations with hardships: five years of high school without lunch or eating breakfast, persevering days without the proper running shoes. The rejection from classmates and worse my teachers was the hardest for me, poverty can be isolating, but I never let it hold me back. Hardships never hindered me from achieving my goals, and I told myself this here is just one more obstacle to my greatness. I fell wholeheartedly on the faith of my mother. Mine was not yet cultivated to withstand this deep uncertainty.

******

It is evening now. Doesn't Auntie C know that the place is unsafe? How could she be so indifferent to my plight? She always told me to get home early because anyone not behind closed doors at 9 PM could be raped or killed.

The one-bedroom apartment where I stayed with Auntie C was in a tenement yard. A public kitchen and bathroom served all the occupants living in the four one-bedroom apartments on the compound. The yard was fenced with old corrugated zinc sheeting. Mannings Hill Road is in the heart of Kingston and was known for

El-Shaddai – God Almighty

violence. Late at nights, especially on the weekends, I would hear the popping of guns breaking the night's silence and shots lighting the still darkness of the city. Kingston was hell, and Mannings Hill was one of the doorways to hell.

The sun had faded. The moon slept in a bundle of dark clouds that hung over the community like a thick cloak. The rain tapped a slow rhythmic beat on the zinc roof interrupted only by the tiny splashes of water rolling from the roof unto the pink and white tiles on the verandah floor.

******

Auntie C opened the door to retrieve her patio chair, and my presence startled her. She grabbed me by my arm and shoved me in the rain – "You cannot stay here." She said with steely determination and disgust, so thick, they were impenetrable. Her resolve was great, and I realized all hope to win her over to take me in her home was lost. I watched as she dragged my plan B, my bed, her patio chair and they disappeared inside the apartment.

I thought about punching her when she grabbed my arm, but I didn't — the first miracle from this wild event. Anyone who knew me back then knows I had the gumption to ball my fist up and hit my aunt. I had beaten up a few boys in All Age School who tried to show me their affection. I had a lot of fight in me. Anyone who knew me knows I could have ripped her to shred with curse words; I could have told her my mind and headed back to Montego Bay. But when God is working a miracle He doesn't just

El-Shaddai – God Almighty

give you good material gifts; He transforms the heart and mind of the receiver.

The anger I know I should be feeling warped into pity. Not pity for me but my aunt. I had no clue what my feeling was about because I was the one standing in the rain with no place to sleep.

I submitted to the feeling of kindness and love that washed over me, and I had no evil thoughts toward my aunt. These feelings were not mine; at least they didn't come from my conscious self.

******

Rain is a good thing, it signifies new growth and cleansing, but at that moment I didn't care for further growth and cleansing…cleansing from what? I am 17, only 17 and needed my mother or a caring adult and a place to rest. I couldn't call my mother, no one in the yard had a phone, and my mother didn't have a phone to accept a call.

A 17-year-old needs cleansing – I needed the rain and God's transformative power, I wasn't done growing. I hadn't even started the journey of my life.

When God wants to build us up, He sometimes takes us away from the comfort of the places we know and the people on whom we are relying. Look at Joseph - he was sold into slavery by his brothers, taken away from his loving father but was later promoted to a leadership role in Egypt where he saved millions from starvation.

But I am not Joseph, and I wondered how God could have taken me this far from home and left me stranded in

El-Shaddai – God Almighty

Kingston, trapped in the middle of the night with no one to care for me and no place to rest my head. I hummed a tune we sang in church while the rain mingled with my tears, *"I just can't give up now. I've come too far from where I've started. Nobody told me the road would be easy. And I don't believe he brought me this far to leave me."* (Mary Mary). Singing was my way of seeking comfort and drawing closer to God. Singing, like prayer, quiets the soul and brings you closer to the Divine; in the book of 2 Kings chapter 3 verse 15 the prophet Elisha said, "But now, bring me a harpist." "And while the harpist played, the hand of the LORD came upon Elisha."

******

Miss Rena, one of the neighbors who shared a one bedroom with her husband, Denis, and two daughters, Sunshine and Bibby, saw what transpired. Miss Rena assumed that whatever disagreements we had would be reconciled before night approached, so she never got involved. As a mother of two, she could not leave me to stand in the rain with no place to go. Her heart melted, and she invited me to sleep on her veranda.

Hope returned!

Miss Rena's wooden chair was not the comfort of Auntie C's bed or even her patio chair, but it felt like a life jacket on the sinking Titanic ship, my life. I was in survival mode, craving some normalcy, and food, I hadn't eaten for more than 12 hours. My family never had much but we always had a place to sleep. I am

El-Shaddai – God Almighty

from a house filled with children but never felt unloved by either parent. Here I am, unloved, unwanted by a relative, the very person whom my parents entrusted with my care.

The night of October 26, 1987 opened my eyes to the cruelty of adults, but I also saw care and love from strangers, the kind my parents gave. The presence of God is always near, and that night I felt the transformative, comforting power of the Divine in a mighty, personal way.

I sat on the wooden patio chair and sang worship songs, I want to share this one with you –

"When trouble is in my way
I can't tell my night from day
When I'm tossed from side to side
Like a ship on a raging tide
I don't worry I don't fret
My God has never failed me yet
Troubles come from time to time
But that's all right,
I'm not the worrying kind because
I've got confidence
God is gonna see me through
No matter what the case may be
I know He's gonna fix it for me..."
(Andraé Crouch)

I know the Divine was on my side. I had faith even in the storm. Mama told me to give thanks to God for the little things, and He will bless me.

It is in the depths of sorrow where you will experience

El-Shaddai – God Almighty

God's greatest miracles. In Sunday school I learned about God saving children from the acts of wicked adults, some were even family members but always people with power – three Hebrew boys in the burning furnace, David and King Saul, Daniel in the Lion's den, and Joseph, sold into slavery by his brothers. These were all children, and God protected them from evil. I trusted the Divine would do the same for me.

I had my bag with my notebooks and other school apparatus in my lap, the bag with my clothes rested on the concrete. I had all I needed to be great.

The dogs were running around the yard, at times whimpering as if they were in pain. I was in their place on the veranda, and they felt displaced. I was happy to have the dogs around; they made me feel safe.

I squinted through the glare of the darkness; it was so thick I could feel it if only I had tried. The winds howled and hurled hands full of water on my feet and spewed cold sprinkles on my face. The zinc fence rattled, and the trees groaned as the wind rustled their leaves.

I consoled myself; this here is better than sitting on the bus going back to Montego Bay. I had faith and faith always attracts hope. The rain started to beat like bullets, rushing in on the shallow floor, and so I placed both bags in my lap. The water swooped in and covered my feet, and I pulled them up on the chair to prevent damaging my shoes. The rain slapped against the sides of the house, now my entire body was washed by the rain. Around 3AM, Ms.

El-Shaddai – God Almighty

Rena opened the door and said –

"Come in; we can't leave yu out here."

I hoped without gain that my aunt would look out just once to see that I was fine, but she never did. I pulled the chair inside the already crowded bedroom, and before I fell asleep I had several small chats with God –

"God do not leave me now I need you more than ever."

"God you started me on this journey, and you will take me to the finish line."

"Protect me O God. Send your angels to guard me."

"Provide for me. Give me a place to rest my head."

"God if you help me I will help the poor."

******

Early Tuesday morning, I got up, showered, and took the bus to college with all my possessions. None of my friends knew of my plight; I looked like I did any other day. I prayed throughout the day for God to help me. My last class ended at 6:45 PM. I ran through the puddles of rain to the bus stop. Several classmates were waiting on their bus, including a young lady with whom I had attended community college in Montego Bay. In desperation I asked
–   "Do you know anyone who needs a boarder?"

I didn't ask a specific person; I just threw my question in the air hoping it would land somewhere safe. Jackie, the young lady from my hometown, responded –

"Yes, the place where I am staying. One of the boarders left on Sunday, and they need someone to

El-Shaddai – God Almighty

replace her."

Jackpot! I shouted in my mind. But I have a problem, I do not have any money, and my parents do not have any money. But this did not stop me from boarding the bus with Jackie, and we headed to Sunrise Crescent to find accommodation.

God has a sense of humor, amid the rain during my dilemma God is taking me to Sunrise Crescent and the night before I slept in a room with a young lady named Sunshine. I wish I had seen the message of hope at the time.

When we got inside the home, Jackie introduced me to the homeowner, Grandma Hutchinson. She was a short, plump, dignified, woman in her late sixties. She wore a warm, friendly smile. Her home reminded me of the place where Mama worked as a helper. I put on my bravest voice, but any adult could see that I was scared –

"Miss, I need a place badly. My aunt put me out, and I need to move in tonight."

Oh no. I shouldn't have told Grandma Hutchinson that my aunt put me out. What if she thought I was a wild girl. An aunt would not just put a teenager out without a good reason. But then Grandma looked me up and down, and she smiled.

"How old are you?"

"17 Miss."

I knew what she thought so I added,

"My mother will send the money."

El-Shaddai – God Almighty

Grandma Hutchinson ignored my second comment.

"You can have the room, but I cannot rent to any teenager. You have to get your mother here."

I was disappointed and happy at the same time. I asked Grandma Hutchinson if I could use her phone to get a message to my parents, she agreed. I paid her a small fee for the call. I was overjoyed when Glen answered his phone. I told Glen what had happened and to pass on the message to Mama –

"I cannot stay with Auntie C, but I found a place to board. I need Mama to meet Grandma Hutchinson before I can move in. Mama must know that I need a place urgently. She had to come to Kingston tomorrow. And she must bring $350.00. Tell her to meet me at the bus terminus in downtown. I will be waiting there."

That night I felt relief. I was happy for myself as well as Ms. Rena and Mr. Denis, I had just fallen upon them like unscheduled rain, and I didn't want to be another problem they had to solve in their already overburdened life. I was thrilled to let them know that I found a place and I would be moving off their verandah on Wednesday.

By the time I returned to Mannings Hill Road, the rain had subsided. I slept on the verandah as if I was in my own bed. Wednesday morning, I called Glen from a public phone. He told me the time Mama's bus was scheduled to arrive. I gathered my bags, thanked Ms. Rena and Mr. Denis, and headed to the bus terminus. I waited for five

El-Shaddai – God Almighty

hours until Mama arrived around 3 PM.

Mama had borrowed the money for my boarding, Grandma Hutchinson loaned me bedlinen, and Wednesday night I slept in Grandma Hutchinson's house after eating a meal of meatballs and spaghetti for dinner that Grandma had prepared for me.

******

Jackie's parents gave her a car after I moved to Sunrise Crescent and for two years I never paid for transportation to attend classes or to visit my home in Montego Bay during the holidays. All the money that I didn't use for bus fare to and from college helped to pay for board and food. But I still could not buy my textbooks. All my years in college I bought three books, Terry Lucy Cost Accounting, Philip Kotler Marketing, and my first-year math book. Before I moved to Sunrise Crescent, I stayed at the library and did my assignments, but that meant traveling the dangerous roads late at nights. Now I was in the comfort of a loving home, and I could borrow Jackie's books whenever she wasn't using them.

Looking back, if Auntie C had not closed the door, I probably wouldn't have finished college. I got more than a college education; God placed me in a home where I had new experiences, shaping me for a future that I couldn't have imagined for myself.

The pressures we face in life are not intended to destroy us but to deliver us. Diamonds, the most sought-after, precious stone is brought to the surface by deep-

El-Shaddai – God Almighty

source volcanic eruptions. Those two nights sleeping on Ms. Rena's patio chair was the beginning of many volcanic eruptions that God would use to mold me over the years.

******

Remember Mr. Denis and Ms. Rena? I haven't seen them since 1991, but uncle Stenford told me they bought a house and are living comfortably. Remember that God does not relinquish His promises and He promised to bless those who help the poor.

What about Auntie C and my uncle? They never had children of their own, and now I have the pleasure of supporting them. They are living in my home in Jamaica.

During a chat with my uncle, he was overwhelmed by the scars of the past, and he wept bitterly. He was carrying a heavy burden and didn't know how to put it down. I tried to help him. I told him that because Auntie C agreed for me to stay with her, she gave me hope. I also reminded my uncle of his kindness towards me, during my years in high school when he bought my textbooks.

"Uncle I am not doing you a favor, you are now reaping from the seeds that you planted".

"My niece, I wish I had planted more."

My uncle's response is one of the more profound statements I have ever heard, and I have tattooed it on my heart.

Your pain and your blessings are not only yours to keep, they should be shared to lift others. God has blessed me so that I can bless others. Since 2003, my family has

El-Shaddai – God Almighty

supported hundreds of children with meals, transport to school, clothes, money, sending children to summer programs. We also provide groceries for the elderly. How could I not give to those in need when I have received so much from the Divine? Like Joseph, God saved me to help others.

What a mighty God we serve! I am happy for closed doors and rejoice when the answer to a prayer is no. Do not be disappointed over that missed opportunity, the love that got away, the job of your dreams that slipped through your fingers. My God, Your God, Our God has extraordinary plans for your life. *"No eye has seen, no ear has heard, no heart has imagined, what God has prepared for those who love Him."* 1 Corinthians 2 verse 9.

******

Learn to forgive.
Plant seeds of kindness.
Give thanks, even in the difficult times.
God blesses those who give to the poor.

El-Shaddai – God Almighty

5

I've Got a Mansion

*Ask and it will be given to you; seek and you will find; knock and the door will be opened to you. For everyone who asks receives; he who seeks finds; and to him who knocks, the door will be opened....*Matthew 7 verses 7-8.

This house could not be from God! My heart sank when Mark pulled up to what seems like an abandoned house and turned off the car's ignition. He was excited like a kid going to see Santa Claus. Mark was filled with great ideas about the potential of the place. But I knew this wreck was not what God had promised me.

God promised me a home. My husband took me to a 300 square feet, ill-shaped box that government contractors had slapped together and had incorrectly labeled it as a house. The cheap limestone wash used as a substitute for paint had yellowed with age and peeled in several places revealing the prefabricated concrete structure. The red metal windows which broke the monotony of the white-washed walls were dated and shut tight as if to keep the darkness in and the sunshine out. The front door bounded tightly with vines shouted – do not enter. The yard was a wild forest, evidenced by the bleating of goats roaming in

El-Shaddai – God Almighty

the back-yard. With grass and weeds five feet tall forming the sound evidence this house could not be from God. Mark's idea of a home was an eyesore, a conglomerate of disappointments.

I refused to consider anything positive about this place. I turned my back and headed to the car signaling my resignation from further discussions, and for Mark to take me home. Mark asked me to pray just one more time.

******

After gunmen attacked our home in Irwin Heights, I was traumatized and could not return. My parents were gracious and kind to Mark and me and allowed us to move in with them. It was good to be home with my parents, but it wasn't ideal. Dada took on the task of finding us a suitable place to live. He was uncomfortable as he watched us looking at homes that either made you laugh or cry in disbelief.

One of the places we viewed was in the heart of the city, Thompson Street. Once a coveted residential area now a mixture of family homes, and small businesses. The owner of the place, an older gentleman, was excited to show us around. You could see the excitement in his eyes when he spoke about the kitchen; it was his pride and joy. What a surprise we got! Right in the middle of the kitchen was the bluest toilet I had ever seen. There was the stove, the fridge, the cupboards, and the blue, working, flushable toilet in the center of the kitchen on a platform. Who puts a toilet in their kitchen? It was practically a throne, with three

El-Shaddai – God Almighty

steps to get to it.   After that day, Dada took on the house hunting for us.

******

Mark and I were delighted when Dada found the two-bedroom apartment on Austin Avenue. Our new home was ideal, the house was only a five-minute walk to my parents' house and it was in a quiet, peaceful neighborhood.

Life has come full circle. As a little girl, I dreamed of living in this very neighborhood. On Sunday evenings Mama and her best friend, Andrea, took a few children on 'Sunday Evening Walks.' Our Sunday Evening Walks were long and lazy, taking us through every breathtaking corner of Austin Avenue. We gazed with amazement at the magnificent homes, with their elegant gardens, and manicured lawns. We took a little piece of Austin Avenue back with us, the flowers planted in the old paint cans on our steps, were our secret gains from the Sunday Evening Walks.

Our new landlord, Mrs. Jones, knew my parents for more than 20 years. Mrs. Jones lived on the upstairs of the building, and we lived in the downstairs apartment, with separate entrances. We settled in and lived there for a full two years without any major incidence.

******

A year after moving to Austin Avenue, our son was born.   Our future was imminent with two children to consider.   Those evenings when life freed us from chores and late hours at work, we chatted about buying a house.

El-Shaddai – God Almighty

Nothing grand, just a place where our children could grow up and call home. It was only a dream. We had no money and no connections to make such a massive purchase. I was 24 years old with two young children and we had no savings. Buying a house anytime soon would have taken a miracle.

Comfort built on material things is fragile and August 1994 my comfort in a rented house came crumbling down. I learned that our plans to buy a home for our family was a criminal offense and my landlord was furious.

Mrs. Jones carefully choose her time to launch an attack, the morning when Mark left for a business trip. I lingered on the verandah a bit to enjoy the early morning breeze and to watch Mark's car until it was out of sight. Without Mark to defend me, Mrs. Jones rained bloody, bitter, and brazen curse words on me. I was shocked and couldn't believe the negative words above were intended for me. The uncertainty evaporated when I heard –

"oonu young bout oonu want fi buy house, red yeye. Tek onnu time. Onnu know how long it tek me fi build dis."

Mrs. Jones cursed at me; she accused me of wanting too much too soon. She thought Mark and I were too young to be thinking about buying a house. How could Mrs. Jones think about our plans of home ownership as being audacious? She did, and she would make us pay.

I should have ignored her but instead, I engaged her as forcefully as she attacked, and I shouted back with harsh,

El-Shaddai – God Almighty

hurtful, and hard-hitting words. My response enraged her more. In the early morning, two women engaged in a silly but bitter exchange of words about a house that was only a dream.

Mrs. Jones had passed by our living room window and overheard our dreams. As much as we were both employed, and I had started a bookkeeping business on the side, we did not have the money to buy a home, we were barely making it from month to month.

Most, if not all, our realities started as a dream, don't they? And my landlord suspected our dream of home ownership might come true and it displeased her. I am still perplexed when I see envy in another human being. What causes jealousy in the human heart? Is it fear? I am still searching for the answers. I wished she knew the pie of life gets bigger each time another person's life improves.

A few weeks after the bruising exchange of words, Mrs. Jones delivered on her promise; we were going to pay for what she conceived was barefaced presumptuousness. We received a legal notice from the courts to vacate the premises by October 31, 1994. In thirty days, we must leave. Since we had no money for the deposit to buy a house, we started to search for another place to rent. We searched tirelessly and couldn't find an affordable house or one in a safe neighborhood.

******

While we were dreaming about buying a house, I never prayed for a house and we didn't search for a home. Now, I

El-Shaddai – God Almighty

didn't have a dream; I have an immediate need. Mark took to the streets to search for a place to rent and I turned to God in prayer for a favor.

Could it be that God forces us to live the abundant life by turning the hearts of our coconspirators to mediocrity against us? Did God turn Mrs. Jones heart against us? Proverbs 21 verse 1 says, *"The king's heart is a waterway in the hand of the LORD; He directs it where He pleases."*

During one of my prayers, I heard the response from the Divine Creator –

"You will not live in another rented house."

"What? Am I hearing clearly?"

"You will not live in another rented house."

I didn't question how this would happen. I knew it was the voice of God and I've come to learn that with God all things are possible. I gave God thanks for His provision.

I told Mark what I heard. Praying for a house was too radical for him. Mark grew up in the countryside where he lived an idyllic life. Not rich but Mark always had food to eat: delicious mangoes, juicy oranges, fresh milk, and freshly laid eggs. On the other hand, my life was filled with scarcity and heavy reliance on God.

I had faith in God to provide our own home, so I started to pack away household items and pieces of clothing that we didn't need immediately. Faith without work is vanity. Mark couldn't understand my faith and he laughed at me for packing. *"Faith the substance of things*

El-Shaddai – God Almighty

hoped for the evidence of which is not yet seen." Hebrews 11 verse 1.

Mark had his own plans - he was going to the courts to fight the order and show Mrs. Jones she cannot just give us notice without a cause. But when God gets ready, we must move.

September came and ended, and we did not find a place to rent and God did not give us a home or the resources to buy one. I still had my faith. God's timing is not ours and God is never late or too early. In the book of Isaiah 60 verse 22, God told his people that He would give them His promises timely and quickly. *"The least of you will become a thousand, and the smallest a mighty nation. I am the LORD; in its time I will accomplish it quickly."*

******

One evening Mark came home excited. He heard about a rental property and there was a possibility we could purchase the house. Mr. Davis, the owner, was renting the place and was also thinking about selling it. Mark's excitement was contagious, and I too got excited and started to thank God without seeing the place. I even began to laugh at Mark and I jeered him –

"What did I tell you?" "God is going to provide a house. We are not renting another place."

Mark had gone to the house before and now it was my turn to check it out. I drove to Farm Heights with an optimistic attitude and a heart filled with gratitude before I even had a glimpse of the property. I believed in God.

And then I saw the house.

******

There is no way God in His right mind would give this to me. Wouldn't God give me a mansion with a shiny gate and staircase like the houses you see on TV? God would never give me a 300 square feet home with vines running all over the windows and the doors.

The Government constructed these houses in the 1980s to give civil servants an opportunity to own their own home. The houses were cheaply built, thrown together by less than honorable workers. The bulging walls ripped in several places exposed the corrugated wires in the belly of the building. The columns forming the foundation were sturdy but were roughly thrown beneath the building. The thin, Celotex ceiling sagged acutely, succumbing to gravity.

My hopes collapsed. Where is my God? Where is the house that He promised me? I told Mark this could not be the house. He had wasted my time. Didn't he know my Father God had only good things in store for me? Sure, God has only good things for us. Good is defined in diverse ways, beautiful and massive or a house we could afford.

We went home. Me babbling about God's promises and Mark listening, listening to God and me. When we got home, Mark said to me in his most gentle husband voice,

"Michelle, pray to God and ask Him to show you the promise."

******

I slumped onto the edge of the bed, closed my eyes,

El-Shaddai – God Almighty

and prayed to God to give me understanding and directions.

"Go back and look at the house again, go back and look the house again."

For the second time, we were back in the car heading to Farm Heights to look at a house I knew wasn't from God and I would never call home. When we got there, the same voice said –

"Ask Mark to pull the vines from the door."

"Mark, pull the vines from the door."

I was hoping that with some miracle the vines were the only reason I hated this place. Mark pulled the vines, revealing a door with brown marks where the vines had wrapped itself. The house was the same ugly house even without the wild bushes covering the entrance.

But something clicked in my heart and flipped my reality. I can only say that God gave me new eyes; I saw my home, the promise from God. I didn't see the ugly house squatting on its rugged foundation. I could see us living in the house, having fun, and raising my children. I became excited. I walked around the house, waded through the five-feet high weeds and saw all the land. We had a couple of fruits trees and lots of space where the children could play.

Reality hit me; we do not have any money. Even this humble home we cannot afford. The house was on the market for 770,000 Jamaican dollars. Mark approached Mr. Davis and told him of our interest in the house. Mr. Davis informed him there was someone else who was also interested in buying the house, but we could meet with him at his home to discuss it. He is a businessman who doesn't get home until late evenings and for two weeks we visited the Davis' and sat on their verandah for hours only to hear him reject our offers. I knew that he had the keys to my promise. His rejections did not shake my faith, they were invitations to return the next evening. I was moving to Farm Heights and Mr. Davis had no choice but to give us the key.

I prayed daily for God to bless us with Farm Heights and I thanked the Divine for His provision. As I packed our belongings, I sang this song –

"He will do it again, he will do it again, just take a look at where you are now and where you have been. He will always come through for you he is the same now as then (God never change) you may not know how you may not know when, but he will do it again."
(Shirley Caesar)

I knew in my heart that God was going to make way for us to leave Austin Avenue and move into my home at Farm Heights. I didn't know how but I knew it would be soon.

We shared our problem with one of our clients, the Fergusons; we provided bookkeeping services for their asphalt and construction company. Mrs. Ferguson and her husband, Evon, paid us two years' fee in advance, J$60,000 and Mark got J$20,000 advance from his boss. We now had J$80,000 dangling carrots to show Mr. Davis; maybe

El-Shaddai – God Almighty

he will be interested in entertaining us now.

******

Our problem was compounded after Mrs. Davis told us the lady we passed outside her gate in the evenings had sold her truck and had most of the cash to pay for the house. She wanted the same thing that I wanted, and she had the resources to get it. After learning who the lady was and what she possessed, I felt nervous when I saw her. I had to pray about my feelings of inadequacy. She might have the cash, but I was carrying a promise from God. After praying, I was more confident and relinquished all concerns. I resolved it in my heart that I would be happy for her even if she were given preference over our offer. God doesn't reside where evil persists, *"For where envying and strife is, there is confusion and every evil work. James 3 verse 16.* God is love and perfect love casts out all fears.

The lady sat in her vehicle and waited, but she always left before Mr. Davis reached home. Mark and I choose to sit on the verandah and chatted with his wife, while we waited on God, and Mr. Davis to arrive. We stayed until he came home ate his dinner and could talk with us.

During one of our chats, we made our best offer; it was ridiculous and laughable – we would give the Davis' J$80,000 as a deposit and then pay rent until we could get a loan to pay the remainder, J$690,000.   Loans in Jamaica could take a long time to process, so this was no real deal for Mr. Davis. He rejected our offer. I kept praying and Mark continued to pursue Mr. Davis. Eventually, we were

El-Shaddai – God Almighty

the only contender. The lady with the cash stopped showing up and gave us more leverage.

******

You would think that because God had promised us this house that we wouldn't need to work so hard, but the scripture said we must knock before the door could be opened. And so, we knocked on the hearts and consciences of Mr. Davis and his wife.

October 29th, Mrs. Davis promised us she would talk with her husband to ensure we get the house. We gave her the cash without a receipt. I prayed while Mark arranged the trucks. We packed the remainder of our belongings trusting in God. October 30, 1994, we went to the Davis' home to collect the key to our home. At midnight October 30, 1994, Mr. Davis handed us the keys and said these words that confirmed that Farm Heights was from God –

"Only God could make me give you my keys."

If only he knew he was confirming what I had known for a few weeks. Who but God? Who else? Who else can make a way when there is none. We packed our belongings and moved into our home on October 31, 1994. Mark had gotten an extension from the courts, we did not have to leave our rented apartment but when God provides a home for you why wait. I wouldn't wait another day to move into the promised land. O how sweet it is to trust in God. We asked, and God answered, we knocked, and God opened the door.

God gave us a 300 square feet home where we held

El-Shaddai – God Almighty

Christmas parties, entertained friends, and even sheltered a friend who was running away from her abusive husband.

******

A promise from God doesn't mean you will receive the promise immediately. Neither does it mean that you will receive the promise without work on your part. We must accept that we are co-creators with God: we must ask, we must seek, we must knock. While we are doing the work, we are creating connections with nature and the people around us. Mark and I created a connection with Mrs. Davis on those long evenings when we chatted with her. She got to see our hearts and she opened hers to us. It was not just a transaction we made a connection.

Too many times our projects fail because we went in for the product and forget the people and the process. Miracles come through a process of connecting and caring for the people around us and protecting nature.

******

God only gives good and perfect gifts to His children, even the tiny, rugged home. What I have come to see and understand over the years is – when we give thanks for the small things, they bring us deep unmeasured joy. Gratitude is a powerful catalyst in the world of miracles.

Gratitude multiplies your gift exponentially and those who watched you and the offering of love will be amazed at what it produced and continues to provide. With thanksgiving, the rugged unsightly thing can become the centerpiece of beauty in your life. Its transformative

El-Shaddai – God Almighty

powers will go on into the ages touching lives and generating beauty in whoever chooses to gaze upon it, not for what it could be but for accepting it for what it is.

Farm Heights was a blessing to my two older children who grew up in that house. They often remarked that they had their happiest memories in Farm Heights. They climbed trees in the backyard, sailed down the hill on their bicycles, and more importantly they learned to be content with whatever God gave us and not to envy what others have. While my children were too young to know the details of how we bought the house, I have shared with them the mighty acts of God.

We lived in Farm Heights for nine years then God provided a mansion in a community that was not even in my dreams. Another miracle. In the book of Ephesians, Paul told the people that God can do substantially more than they could ever ask for or even imagined. For me to move to Coral Gardens in my own home, 5,000 square feet with marble floors is part of what Paul was telling the people of God. And my story is not even finished.

Twenty years later, in 2014, we sold Farm Heights to make the down payment for a home that was 32 times larger. Our rugged home had increased in value by nearly 1000%. In 2014 the ugly house allowed me to buy the home I thought I should have gotten in 1994. I shared with my children that it was Farm Heights that provided the deposit for my current home. My son said –

"Mommy this is like the feeding of five thousand with

El-Shaddai – God Almighty

five fish and two loaves."

It was a God moment for me. I thanked God that He opened the eyes of my child to understand the power of what He had done for us and I hope He will do the same for anyone reading this. God makes the impossible possible.

******

There are times in our lives when we cannot accept the beautiful gifts that God has given to us because we dislike the package - jobs, spouse, homes, cars, children. Instead of receiving our blessings with grace, we look at what others have and compare our gifts to theirs. And if in our eyes we do not get what we wanted we set out to direct the hand of God to give us things that will fill our egos and make others think more highly of us. What God gives us is more than good enough, it will blossom and provide long term benefits, benefits we cannot predict.

God is not impressed by packages He is about giving us the things we need to grow, the things we need to have an abundant life. God will never give us things that will be albatrosses over our lives nor things that will lead us into temptation.

El-Shaddai – God Almighty

Look around in your life today and give thanks for all the things that God has given you. Even the unsightly one. God only gives good gifts to His children.

******

Ask, Seek, Knock, and Accept.
Gratitude is a multiplier.
Connect with people.
Do not curse the gift because of an unsightly wrapping.

El-Shaddai – God Almighty

God Protects

Jehovah Tsaba

The Lord our Warrior
"The LORD is a warrior, the LORD is His name." Exodus 15
verse 3

6

Ricochet

"So, they hanged Haman on the gallows he (Haman) had prepared for Mordecai...." Esther 7 verse 10

Fights between the boys in the community were the daily rhythms of their teenage years, common as breathing and moved with the ebbs and flow of their changing moods. There was sure to be a fight after every football match, one boy cheated, and another played too rough. These fights ended as quickly as they started. The boys' love for football and their need for each other to create fun were enough to referee all their fights. Parents rarely got involved, and if they did it was to discipline all the boys. The rhythm of this peace was disrupted after the 1980 general when illegal guns proliferated the streets of the ghetto

******

The power of owning this piece of metal shifted something in these young boys. The guns replaced their need for friendships with the need to be a Don – the leader of everyone, someone to be feared and respected. The gun was powerful, and power corrupts even little boys.

The nightly news was a summary of body counts –

Jehovah Tsaba – God Protects

lives taken by guns. A few years before, I saw the power of the bullet as it silenced the laughter of my classmate seconds before the echoes of its sound disappear and the smoke settled.

At 11 years old, I never knew any boy from the community who was in a gang neither did I know anyone with a gun. This was until Mama's church sister stopped by our gate declaring that her son was about to kill my brother in retaliation for kicking her son in a game of football.

******

I was terrified. Food tasted like paper, and I couldn't sleep at nights. I had dreams of my brother laying in a pool of blood. The death threats tossed over the fence by Mama's church sister kept looping in my head –

"Yu tink your son dem bad? Me son gwaan kill dem. Him a go blow off dem head!!"

She cursed at the top of her lungs, flayed her arms, and shook her entire body – in full display of her power. She eventually walked away, but she continued her cursing, a flagrant display of her strength. Her words echoed in the vacuum of silence created by the terror she had generated with her rage. It wasn't enough for our neighbors to hear her threats; she wanted everyone she encountered to know that she was powerful and should be respected. She clambered through the dusty lane, back to her own home.

This was unusual. Parents, especially church-going mothers, usually talk things out. Mama was eager to reason with her church sister, but she would have nothing to do with peace. She was certain that whatever my brother did to her son warrants the ultimate price, my brother's life. The gun gave a destructive voice to my mother's church sister and it silenced the God within. It was then that I understood that power without love for others is destructive and creates the archetypical structure for evil to survive. Mama's church sister had forgotten the power of love and prayer, but Mama didn't. Mama went to God in prayer in the privacy of her bedroom. I caught a brief glimpse of her heart before she left to pray, and it was knitted with worry, and cold, dark horror.

******

I could not hear the words of Mama's prayer, but her sobs filtered through the cracks of the wooden frame that separated us. Mama was a wounded animal, whimpering and sobbing, she was weak and helpless. My heart burned red with rage against that woman and soft with pity for Mama.

I've seen God provide food for my family, God restored my baby brother to good health when doctors had sent him home to die, even the house that we owned was a miracle from the Divine. Could God protect us from a young man with a gun and a mother without a fit conscience? I know Mama said God could do all things, but I do not think He can handle an impending murder.

The quiet sobbing from Mama's place of prayer evolved into triumphant shouting – "Thank you, Jesus.

Jehovah Tsaba – God Protects

Mama was shouting for Jesus, clapping her hands, and giving thanks. Our lives were still in danger; why is she thanking God? Is Jesus going to send an army to deliver my brother and my family?

I never asked Mama what she prayed; it was of no interest and frankly I thought it was useless. When Mama emerged from the secret place of her bedroom, I couldn't look at her. I am afraid to look at desperation and brokenness. She called my brother –

"Come here, me need fi talk wid yu."

My brother came through the front door of the living room; his lanky frame caved in from the looming threat of his death, a death he could taste. I knew he was worried because later that evening he was asking my parents to send him to the country to stay with my grandfather.

"Did you kick your friend?"

"No Mama, we were only playing football."

"No tell me no lie or you going to pay. Yu understand me?

"Yes, Mama. We were playing."

My brother could not have understood the gravity of what Mama was talking about. None of us who heard her prayer believed God could put an end to this threat.

Mama asked him again, and his response was the same. She sat back down in the spot where the death threats were hurled at her and said,

"It is finished."

Mama's words and actions carried a kind of secret

power that made me scared. As nosey as I was, I was too afraid to find out what, 'it is finished' meant. There are times words carry such weight that it need no interpretation to reveal its meaning.

As I juxtapose the different positions taken by Mama and her church sister, I see the same pattern in the lives of so many people; when life is good and things are going great, God is placed on the shelf. But when trouble comes they run to God for help. We often treat God as a miracle ATM or the Genie in a bottle. Mama's church sister got it all wrong, we always need God.

Mama continued to pray for our daily protection. Her prayers weren't enough to reassure me of my brother's safety, and so I waited for his death with dreadful anticipation. The nightly news of young men being murdered in surrounding communities didn't help; each report brought the harsh reality of death's sting closer to my heart.

******

The power of the gun, taker of life, was no match for God, the Giver of life.

He was a handsome boy with a beautiful chiseled face and almond-shaped eyes that stood out against his dark, flawless skin. Only a teenager but carried away by the power of the gun and feckless mother who could not direct his path.

******

Jehovah Tsaba – God Protects

On a sunny Friday afternoon, my brother's friend was getting his weapon ready for his next 'mission'. As the sun set in the west of the island and left the bright orange trail in the clouds, the gun went off. There was one last bullet that he had forgotten to remove. The explosion shattered the activities of the evening and was heard several streets away from his house — one blow to his forehead. There was no saving him. He was just a child; he never got a chance to experience the full joys of life. When I heard of his passing, I felt safer, but I was deeply saddened.

Was my brother the target of his Friday night mission? Who knows, that knowledge was buried with the young man.

******

Evil and good, whatever we do, comes right back to us. Do not fear your enemies, anything that they are doing to you; they have already done to themselves. Do you have an evil boss, a disagreeable neighbor, a family member or a friend whose mission in life is to bring you sorrow? Do not worry, the Divine has set a natural law in order, and they will reap the pain that they thought they were sowing for you.

"Depart from evil and do good; Seek peace and pursue it."
Psalm 34 verse 14

******

**Do not seek to fight your battles by yourself.
Standstill and watch God fight your battles.**

Jehovah Tsaba – God Protects

7

Guns and Roaches

1 Samuel 17 verse 45 "Then said David to the Philistine, you come to me with a sword, and with a spear, and with a shield: but I come to you in the name of the LORD of hosts, the God of the armies of Israel, whom you have defied."

We slept in a veil of ignorance while tragedy loomed over our community. The daylight fell asleep releasing its dark shadows, giving permission for evil to find its way through the seditious darkness that covered the night's sky.

The shadowy frame crouched beneath our bedroom window, gun in his hand, man on a mission, poised to accomplish a horrific task. My husband's life was riddled with question signs. We stood motionless as horror nailed our feet to the wooden floor. I waited for the explosion that would blister the serenity of the night and destroy my world. I wanted to close my eyes, but I couldn't.

How could I watch as he falls? How could I watch his lifeless body hitting the wooden floor where we were just killing roaches? I didn't want to see his life splattered on the blue cinder blocks that protected us while we slept. A thousand thoughts trampled on my mind. I waited for the unthinkable that would sink my world.

******

My job as an auditor took me away from home for more than half of the calendar year. April 1992 was no different. I was away for a week on assignment in Negril at the Charlena Hotel with two colleagues. As auditors, hotel audits were the coveted assignments compared to auditing warehouses and farms. We were treated like royalties and we were in no rush to return home.

Thursday came and with it was the pulsating urgency that nagged me relentlessly. I had this gut feeling calling out for me to head home immediately. It was a strange nagging feeling that something was happening at home that would bring me sorrow. How can I tell what I heard or felt? I really cannot say, but it feels like my soul whispered to my heart with such firmness that I must act and act quickly. The sense of danger was so great, I had the feeling of being suffocated. The feeling crept upon me unsuspectingly and wouldn't leave. Staying until Friday evening was one day too many and so I told my colleagues that something is wrong at home and I had to leave.

I took the chance of really looking crazy, my colleagues knew I had no phone at home and they also knew I hadn't communicated with any family members. I placed my team leader in a precarious position, what would she say to our manager? "Gwen had a strange feeling and had to go home." In a professional world that's loony and I could face disciplinary actions but that didn't cross my mind back then and I wouldn't have cared. I had more pressing needs, getting pass fifty-seven miles from Negril to Montego Bay and up to the hills of Irwin Heights, and to my family.

******

I packed my bags and took the bus. The two-hour journey was filled with prayers, some I cannot recall but I know I asked God to protect my little girl and to cover our home. I recalled asking God to send angels to guard my gates and my doors. I recalled those words because those were the words I heard Mama said to God when I was a little girl and we were in danger. I only had the words that my mother prayed to comfort me on my journey home and a Bible verse that I studied when I was around five years old, *"Believe on the Lord Jesus Christ and you and your household will be saved."* Acts 16 verse 31.

Let me put a parenthesis here to say, my relationship with God was severely neglected, I rarely prayed, my Bible was dormant somewhere in the house, and the last time I went to church was my wedding, five months before. Who needs Jesus when you have everything you need? I had my husband, a college education, a decent job, and a healthy baby. I needed Jesus now and I prayed –

"Jesus, this is me. I know I have neglected you, but you promise you will save me and my family if I believe in you and Jesus I believe in you."

Do you know who need Jesus? The ones who believe they have everything. How else can you be content if the

Giver of good things is not in charge of those good things. I never knew that I was powerless; I was young and foolish. Psalm 127 verse 1 tells us, *"Unless the LORD builds the house, its builders labor in vain; unless the LORD protects the city, its watchmen stand guard in vain."*

******

The two-hour journey felt like an eternity. I was overjoyed when I got home to the sleepy community of Irwin Heights and saw my sister with my baby on her lap. The look on my sister's face told me that something was wrong, but my baby girl was safe in her arms. Who cares what else in the world is wrong if my baby is alive? I rushed to my baby and cuddled her.

My sister described the harrowing events of the day. Three gunmen entered the community around 10 o'clock that morning and moved from house to house with a massive force of destruction. They robbed the residents of their belongings and those who had nothing worth taking they beat them bloody before leaving. My sister was visibly shaken and talking about the incident was a relief for her but brought back the jarring memories.

My sister, Janet, took care of my daughter, Marjanne, while Mark and I went to work. That Thursday, her husband came to visit her. While he was standing at the gate he saw Ray (the gang leader) and his men storming through the neighborhood. Ray was a known criminal in our city and was wanted by the police. Ray always outwitted the law and evaded them. Ray and my brother in law, Earl, lived in the same community and knew each other. I was told that Ray walked up to Earl and said,

"You see me, but you never see me"

Ray placed his index finger to his lips, a warning sign for Earl to keep quiet or else, …. On seeing Earl, they decided, not to enter my home but retreated to other homes where they pillaged and plundered.

I've often wondered about the coincidence of Ray's entrance to the community, who opened the 'gates' and let him in? Or was it a gift that Earl had visited that day? Sometimes our troubles are through association and other times there are no explanations. Nobody died, and so I moved on from the thought of how all of this transpired.

The storm has passed, thieves do not attack the same place twice.

Sunday night we turned our lights out and placed Marjanne to sleep in her crib in the adjoining bedroom. Some nights I would have her sleep with us, but Mark insisted that she sleeps in her own space and that night I agreed.

******

The warm air rushed in from the sea and rustled the leaves, gently caressing the night. It was the right temperature for a relaxing sleep. The pallid strands of light from the silver moon bounced off the glass window panes and leaked through the pink, lace curtains. The street light cast its shadowy frame over my bedroom window as it tried to pierce the thick darkness of the night. Crickets

Jehovah Tsaba – God Protects

interrupted the quiet of the night singing their goodnight lullabies. Soon we were carried away by the sounds and drifted off to sleep.

Buzzzzz, buzzzzz. Mark and I jumped up after about an hour into our sleep. Roaches flying in confusion as if someone had disturbed their nests. There were roaches on our bed, on the floor, on the curtain, flying in the air, bouncing off the walls, they were everywhere, filling every inch of the room. We got into action killing them. When we got the last one we went back to sleep.

No, it wasn't the last one, buzzzzz, buzzzzz. More roaches!! Where did they come from? We have been living in this house for one year and had never seen one roach before and now we had a roach invasion. Roaches were coming from every crevice of the floorboards. Mark and I were on our knees fighting for a little piece of sleep not realizing we were on our knees fighting for our lives, but we didn't know it just yet.

There are times in our lives when God place us on our knees and that is how we survive.

******

Zooooom, crash, bang! A second stone flew like a missile through the window, torpedoing through the air and landed on our bed. The first stone had already cleared the path for the attack and had landed in our daughter's room where it ricocheted off the wall and we later saw that it landed in front of her crib. Large chunks of glass stuck in the bed like shrapnel and tiny shards sprinkled Mark and me like burning rain. I was dazed. I knew we were in danger, but I didn't know how much?

"Jesus! Jesus Christ! Help us!" I quietly prayed.

"Help us, help."

Whatever words I uttered were not audible, my lips were too parched with dread and shock for anything to slip from my mouth. There was pandemonium in the neighborhood. We weren't the only ones under attack.

"Help!! Help!! Thief!! Murder!!" Cries for help coming from neighbors ripped through the warm April night.

POW!!! POW!!!

Shots rang through the night destroying the gentleness of the night's sounds and piercing the peace we had taken for granted. The gunmen separated for the attack, it was like watching hyenas surrounding their prey going in for the kill. Guns in hand gave them confidence, the darkness of the night kept them safe, they walked boldly, and with ease. They looked like men clocking in for the night shift on a routine work day, no rush, no panic.

The only people panicking were their victims. I felt sick, I felt hopeless, and powerless. I couldn't think about myself I could only think about my baby in the next room. In this turmoil she was quiet, too quiet. Wild thoughts that I cannot speak of crippled my mind. Did any of the glass ricocheted and landed in her crib? Oh God keep her alive. The silence from her room pierced my heart, cold.

I watched the gunmen's shadowy frame as they walked

Jehovah Tsaba – God Protects

about the yard as if they were paragons of the night. Anything that moved they could stop it right in its track. Anything that breathes they could snuff out in seconds. They could conquer and possess everything in sight. They walked as if they had all the time in the world to kill us. I was puzzled by their bare-facedness, they never wore masks to disguise themselves, they owned the night.

One group attacked my landlord and the other attacked our house. We heard the painful cries of my landlord's wife.

"O God, O God." I shouted, in my head, "please protect them, please protect us."

Facing danger was melodramatic for me, the past events of my life kept piling on in my mind, flashing faster than the speed of light. I relived my entire 22 years in a matter of seconds. But the present events moved in slow motion.

******

Mark stood by a column inside our bedroom, machete in hand, as he tried to catch a glimpse of the mayhem and the men's location. That is when the leader of the gang, Ray, came up to the window and pointed the gun at him.

"Jesus! Jesus!"

I screamed, the words slipped from my mouth as if I had rehearsed them.

"Jesus! Jesus!"

I shouted again. The words rushing from the depths of my heart where only love resides. The love of my life, my husband, the father of my child was one bullet away from Ray's triggered fingers. Nothing stood between Mark and Ray's bullet, there was no cover for Mark. He was in clear line of sight and was marked for death.

When we call on Jesus, all things are possible. I stood six feet from my husband, separated by our bed. I looked at him and he was looking at Ray and I called out,

"Jesus!" Mama told me, "There is power in the name of Jesus."

And then I heard the sound that I dreaded – Click! There was no pow. Mark froze, he couldn't move not even to save himself. Click again, there was no pow. The gun was stuck! He tried twice but not a bullet could be released from the gun. Now they are going to break in the doors, the thought raced through my mind. And so, I shouted,

"Jesus! Jesus! I need you Jesus."

Ray gathered his men and they fled from our yard. Luke 10:17 *The seventy-two returned with joy, saying, "Lord, even the demons are subject to us in your name!"*

There is power in the name of Jesus. In the name of Jesus, the enemies fled.

******

During times of such great tragedy and uncertainty survival is the only thing on one's mind and we knew staying in this house was false security. The doors and windows were not built for war. We had two choices, face the dark of night and the quiet uncertainties outside the door or stay hopelessly locked in a house with fragile doors

Jehovah Tsaba – God Protects

and shattered windows and wait for daylight to save us. We choose the former. I couldn't think straight, I wasn't thinking but I could follow Mark's directions. In urgent whispers he guided me –

"Pack a bag for Marjanne, we will be heading for the car."

The street light cast a dreary shadow across our bed, I could see the large stone occupying the spaces where Mark and I laid just a few minutes ago. Shards of glass shining like diamonds in the embers of the street light unveil the truth of the danger we barely escaped. I could not feel, I could not think, I could not even say an original prayer.

The 23rd Psalm became my refuge, *"Even though I walked through the valley of the shadow of death I will fear no evil for thou are with me."*

I robotically followed Mark's instructions, I crept on my hands and knees to my baby's room. She was awake and standing in the middle of her crib. She was quiet. Did she sense the danger? There was no shouting for mommy or daddy. Her silence was her own safety and ours. Did God send an angel to calm her? I will say yes, she is a precocious child who wants to know everything, and she shouts for mommy and daddy the minute her eyelids are opened.

I packed a bag for Marjanne while Mark quickly surveilled the yard.

"Oh God she is only 14 months old."

"Please God let her live to go to high school."

I had flashback of a movie I watched when I was six years old. It was about the Vietnam war and the nanny fell on top of a baby and saved her during a bombing scene. I was thinking that if Ray and his gang returned, I would fall on my daughter and save her life too. It is crazy where our minds go in times of danger. What else could I think of? My future was a blank slate, I could only look to the past as an anchor to make sense of life.

I picked up our baby and wrapped her in a blanket and waited for Mark to call me when it was safe. He called. I jumped in the car and we headed to the nearest police station.

******

The policemen went to the community and searched all night without luck. Once again Ray had slipped the lawmen and disappeared in the dark of the night.

I felt violated. I was traumatized. I could not face that house again. We packed our belongings and moved into my parents' house for a few months until we found another place to rent.

Ray didn't change his ways and a year later he was captured by citizens during a robbery attempt. April 1993 he was handed over to the police. It was reported that the vehicle in which he was being transported had a flat tire and while the police were trying to change the tire he tried escaping and was shot. He died on the way to the hospital.

Romans 12 verses 18 and 19 – *If it is possible on your part, live at peace with everyone. Do not avenge yourselves, beloved, but leave room for God's wrath. For it is written: "Vengeance is Mine, I will repay, says the Lord."*

******

Vengeance is the Lord's and He will repay.
There is power in the name of Jesus.

Jehovah Tsaba – God Protects

8

There is Power in Prayer

"....Help me, O LORD my God: O save me according to thy mercy: That they may know that this is thy hand; that thou, LORD, hast done it. Let them curse, but bless thou: when they arise, let them be ashamed; but let thy servant rejoice. Let mine adversaries be clothed with shame, and let them cover themselves with their own confusion, as with a mantle..." Psalm 109

I wanted him dead! And I wanted his death to be speedy. Not only did he physically attacked me, but this young man also wanted to kill my husband, he threatened the future and safety of my family.

******

Prayer is one of the most powerful tools that we have.

Prayer can give life, and prayer can also take away life.

Prayer can be used to bless, and prayer can also be used to curse.

Prayer can build up, and prayer can also tear down.

Jehovah Tsaba – God Protects

Prayer works, and we must be careful how we use it.

Prayer is an integral part of my life. Most of my prayers are for lifting others, seeking God to transform the lives of those who are not aware of the light within. But in June 2004 I prayed a different prayer. It was June 2004 I prayed a prayer I sometimes mourned. I prayed a prayer of doom and death. As I cautioned, prayer must be used responsibly, be careful who you bless and be careful who you curse.

******

My husband, Mark, and I went to the market to purchase ground produce every Saturday. We have never taken the children with us because the market is a difficult place to navigate and can be dangerous. But for all its difficulties, we chose to buy our vegetables and fruits in the market instead of the grocery stores.

The grocery stores were clean and safe, items were neatly stacked on the shelves in their styrofoam containers and plastic wrappers. The packages deceptively hid the rotting fruits and vegetables that could not be returned once you leave the store. The floors were clean, but the smell of antiseptic perfumed the air and the store smelled more like the hospital than a place of healthy desires. The grocery store was a sterile place with suspicious food, and no human connection.

On the other hand, the local market is a hassle, droves of sweating bodies pushing against each other, vendors shouting – "Sweet lady buy some nice mangoes." "Young man, come and look pon me yellow yam."— Shoppers bargaining – "Me nah pay $10 fi dat." "Me will give yu $6."— Vendors without stalls walked through the crowds shouting, "boil eggs, boil eggs." Another one shouting, "peanut soup, hot peanut soup."

Despite the hustle and bustle, and the potential dangers, the market drew us in with its cornucopia of fresh foods, and the friendships we developed. There were bounties of red ripe tomatoes, firm green bananas, juicy fruits like red otaheite apples, green and yellow june plums, stinking toes clothe in their hard-brown shells waiting to be cracked by the children, mangoes of all colors, shapes, and sizes provoking and enticing the taste buds. Trelawny yellow yam, dasheen, breadfruit…

The vendors became our Saturday friends. We knew their children's names, what aches and pains they suffered, plans and dreams they have.

******

The market was also bait for criminal elements looking for their next victims. The dreaded sounds no one wanted to hear often disrupt the commerce of the market – "Thief, thief, thief, kill him, kill him…"

Petty thieves would grab a shopper's purse or run away with a vendor's apron holding the day's sales. The justice in the market was vigilante, if a robber was caught he was attacked and beaten, sometimes to his last breath.

Mark could spot pick-pockets (thieves) miles away, he said that they had a certain walk that made them seem

Jehovah Tsaba – God Protects

nervous and they had darting eyes. His awareness gave me a sense of safety as we pushed our way through the crowds.

******

That Saturday in June 2004, I was a few steps ahead of Mark buying tomatoes. As soon as I walked away from the vendor's stall, I felt a slap in my stomach. I was shocked, so shocked that I couldn't feel the pain that came with the impact of the blow. I spun around only to face my attacker. He was so close that I could feel the sting of his breathe in my nostril. He scowled in my face and a wild sound intentionally escaped his throat as he moved in closer to attack again. He raised his hand as if to strike me one more time and I closed my eyes and prayed a quick prayer, "God, protect me, Jesus save me." I opened my eyes and he had both hands at his side.

He was tall and black as the night with unkempt hair. His shirtless chest revealed a life of hardships, I could see all his bones. The rims of his eyes were red, his lips were chapped and baked with a white crust. He was no more than 21 but he looked like a man who had lived many lives.

He saw the horror that seeped into my being and it made him laugh. Even with laughter, his eyes were cold and saturated with evil. He stepped away from me focusing his attention to Mark. His toothless grin mocked Mark as he slowly swayed in my husband's direction.

His grin got wider daring Mark to come and defend me. I could see his thick red, toothless gum. I saw when he pulled his knife and taunted Mark to come and protect me.

Jehovah Tsaba – God Protects

Mark's steps were not swift enough for him, and Mark wasn't angry enough to take on a fight, so he tried motivating Mark to bring on the fight with harsh curse words,

> "dutty white bwoy me a go kill yu and yu woman. Yu can't defend har. If you come closer me cut out har belly and then cut out fi yu".

Mark stopped!

I could see desperation and hopelessness tied into one strong rope that hung like a noose around my husband's neck, a cord ready to take his life. I started to think about my four children at home – "God they cannot be orphans." And I prayed another quick prayer, "God, please don't let Mark try to defend me."

The young man edged towards Mark, making slow, deliberate steps and brandishing his knife. He was not satisfied with slapping me. He was not fulfilled with the humiliation of my husband, he wanted blood and possibly death. My body froze but my mind went to Psalm 91. I closed my eyes and prayed the words – *"He who dwells in the secret place of the Most High shall abide under the shadows of the Almighty. I will say of the Lord He is my refuge..."*

I opened my eyes before completing the prayer of Psalm 91 and I saw our attacker retreated and walked in the opposite direction.

******

Jehovah Tsaba – God Protects

Mark and I rushed towards each other. Mark held my hands and squeezed it tight. I felt a surge of his pain. His hands were trembling, they were cold and damped. I held them tight and returned the squeeze.

We abandoned our shopping and went home unharmed but emotionally bruised. I felt like the foods in the grocery store, well packaged but damaged where no one could see. I was hurting but not because of the slap. The horror of the attack triggered something inside me that caused my entire body to ache. I would later learned that this was Post Traumatic Stress Disorder, PTSD, from the time when gunmen invaded my community.

I was saddened that no one came to my rescue. I should have screamed and shouted thief, but he wasn't trying to take anything from me, except my life. People didn't value life so much. I guess that's why it is easy to kill a robber... life values less than a day's wages.

I was angry. It has been a long time since I have been this wounded. I prayed a prayer you might be tempted to pray if you have been wronged. I prayed a prayer I have never prayed again. I prayed a prayer that you may judge me for sending out to the Divine.

When I got home and reflected on that young man and how evil filled him. When I thought about his deliberate actions to humiliate and harm I prayed –

"God, do not let the enemy walk victoriously over your children. Take him down, God. I want him dead. I want him dead now!"

Jehovah Tsaba – God Protects

The next Saturday his picture was on the front of the local newspaper. He tried robbing a vendor four days after he attacked us. The woman had a gun and she took him out.

As I grew in Christ and realized that prayers are powerful, I questioned should I have prayed a prayer to change him? I believe the power of the Divine is to build up as well as to destroy.

"In Your mercy cut off my enemies and destroy all those who afflict my soul. For I am Your servant. Psalm 143 verse 12.

******

What a man sows he will reap.

God Provides

Jehovah Jireh

The LORD will provide. He will see our needs and meet them. His Grace is sufficient.

"The poor will eat and be satisfied; those who seek the LORD will praise him may your hearts live forever!" Psalm 22:26

9

Telephone Call to Heaven

You do not have because you do not ask. James 4 verse 2

A day I will never forget. The day I thought my beautiful mother had lost her mind.

Mama stood in the center of the kitchen door, she braced her arms against the wooden frame, and prayed for the impossible. She prayed for meat and waited. I waited with her, and I prayed for her sanity.

When Mama placed the pot on the kerosene stove everything seemed fine, she looked normal and sounded normal too. I was perfectly happy with the flour dumplings that I would have for dinner that night, dripping in melted, salted butter. But now she is gone crazy and is asking God for meat. I wanted to tell her not to worry, but I choose silence. I had a cousin who was hospitalized for mental illness, and whenever we tried talking to him he got violent, so I left Mama to her thoughts.

******

If smoke creaked through the cracks of the wooden shed in the backyard, that was our kitchen, I was perfectly happy. Smoke signaled food. I never cared about the quality. I just wanted something to quiet the rumble in my

Jehovah Jireh – God Provides

stomach.

Smoke was a good thing when Mama was the one creating it. At nights my parents watched the shed for signs of smoke. The shed served as the kitchen during the day and the hang-out spot for my brothers and their friends at nights. My brothers made smoke that carried a strange odor. I would peak in through the broken boards and watched them as they rolled the green leaves in the white paper that ended up looking like cigarettes. They would light one end and placed the other end to their lips and inhaled. When they exhaled, smoke filled the air. Whatever was in their homemade cigarettes made them walk as if they were gliding through the air and gave me a headache. If my brothers made smoke, they would feel the power of Mama's right hand.

******

I enjoyed helping Mama with dinner; we filled the spaces between prepping and cooking with stories about her childhood, and her hopes and dreams for her children. That's how I learned the poem, 'Spanish Needle' by Claude McKay.

"Lovely dainty Spanish needle
With your yellow flower and white,
Dew bedecked and softly sleeping,
Do you think of me tonight?"

I loved listening to Mama recite the Spanish Needle poem. I especially enjoyed how she emphasized the 'Lov' in lovely; it tickled me every time. Knowing that my

Jehovah Jireh – God Provides

mother was once a little girl made her more reachable and made my heart tender towards her. Mama didn't know a lot about the things written in books, but she was wise. She used every moment with her children to teach us all that she knew. I wondered how much more I would have known about life if Mama knew more?

Helping Mama in the kitchen also gave me sweet rewards, I tasted the food throughout the cooking process. I tasted a great deal before dinner was ready. Another sweet joy of mine was kneading the flour for the dumplings, I would accidentally pour too much water in the mixture, and Mama had to put more flour in the batter, more dumplings for everyone.

******

The evenings in the kitchen with Mama held fond memories for me but nothing like the evening when I thought she had lost her mind.

There was nothing particularly special about the afternoon of which I speak. It was an ordinary Jamaican day. The voices of children playing in the lane floated high above the zinc roofs, and their laughter sounded of idle safety. Several flocks of birds flew east, towards the hills. The birds with their shiny black feathers created a magnificent contrast against the white fluffy clouds and the light blue sky. They squawked loudly today as they did yesterday.

In our backyard, the chickens settled in the custard apple tree with their usual fight for space, no different from

Jehovah Jireh – God Provides

the nightly fights between my sister, Janet, and me. We fought every night as we get ready for bed –

"Michelle, don't touch mi wid yu foot dem."

"Janet, yu sticking out yu battam and mek it touch me pon purpose."

We fought like that our entire lives until I left for college.

The boiling dumplings bumped rapidly against the metal pot and pushed against the lid. Dinner would be ready in a few minutes, I could tell by the thickness of the froth that seeped through the pot cover.

After the food was cooked, Mama poured the contents from the steaming black pot into a large red plastic container. She would wrap the stained kitchen towel around the bowl and hurriedly bring it to our living room to feed us.

This evening Mama put the container on the kitchen counter blackened with soot from the kerosene stove. She stood in the frame of the kitchen door, and then she lost her mind. She went crazy. Mama asked God for meat.

I can see it as if it happened just a few minutes ago, Mama in her floral head tie, yellow blouse with red and blue trim around the sleeves, and brown and yellow checkered skirt. She did not look like she belonged in the scene; she was beautiful and powerful, yet there was something gentle and vulnerable about her.

Mama lifted her eyes to hills and asked the impossible. I know she is mad. Mad like my friend's mother who got

Jehovah Jireh – God Provides

deported from the USA. I pray she doesn't strip down to her birthday suit like my friend's mother.

She didn't. She spoke to God as if she was talking to a father who cared for his child and would listen –

"God, all the cattle on the mountainside are yours, and you said you would not give your children stone if they ask you for bread. So tonight, God my children are not going to eat food without meat. God, I am not going inside that house tonight until you send meat."

Surely the toll of taking care of nine children has made her mad. Doesn't she know we want to eat our dinner tonight, it is almost 6 PM? Who is going to leave their home now to bring us meat?

Nobody in our neighborhood could help even if they had overheard her crazy talk and wanted to help God to help us.

******

We waited, ten minutes, then fifteen, it seems like forever, but Mama waited. The last flock of birds chattered as they passed overhead. They seemed to mock us with their loud squawk. If one fell from the sky would Mama consider that an answer to her prayer? Didn't God provide ravens for the Israelites? What about my family and the people on Piggott Street? I prayed for a bird to fall right in our yard, maybe two or three. The birds flew by.

******

My thoughts and hunger were interrupted by the voice of my uncle Ezra calling out –

Jehovah Jireh – God Provides

"Brother Egbert, Sister Gloria!"

At the sound of my uncle's voice, Mama shouted "Thank you, Jesus."

Uncle Ezra is my father's younger brother who lived with us for a few years while he was trying to make life in the city. Uncle was now working as a chef in one of the major hotels in Montego Bay and was earning enough to take care of himself and his parents. Uncle Ezra came bounding around to the back of the house like a giddy young girl in love. I know that feeling now. It's the heart bursting with joy when you are part of something greater than yourself. Giving fills the giver with pleasure.

I saw the bags in his hands before I saw him. Immediately I knew there was meat in those bags. Gratitude and disbelief filled my little heart all at once. Did God hear Mama? How did He act so quickly? This God must care. It seems like Mama had a telephone line to Heaven.

The two large bags were filled with chicken, codfish, beef, pork, oil, thyme, tomato, and fresh herbs. How did my uncle know that we were waiting for him? How could he have known that Mama wanted meat? There is no way for anyone to tell him, no one in our neighborhood had house phones, and mobile phones were not yet a thing.

Mama did not look surprised when she saw uncle straining beneath the weight of the bags. She thanked uncle Ezra as if she had sent him to the store.

Jehovah Jireh – God Provides

******

I have always wondered what Mama would have done if meat never came. In 2013, I asked.

"Me dawta, if meat never come me wudda give God thanks same way. But I had confidence that my God is the Provider and He was going to provide me."

"Therefore, I tell you, whatever you ask for in prayer, believe that you have received it, and it will be yours." Mark 11 verse 24.

******

Ask.

Believe.

Receive.

Prayer is a telephone line to Heaven.

Jehovah Jireh – God Provides

10

Did the Birds Plant the Vegetables?

Then the LORD said to Moses, "I will rain down bread from heaven for you. The people are to go out each day and gather enough for that day. Exodus 16 verse 4

There is a story in the Bible about God sending food from heaven for His people as they traveled through the wilderness. God had taken them out of slavery, and was taking them to the Promised Land. On their way, when they encountered several hardships - hunger and lack of water. God didn't leave them to die; He provided food. This strange new food was called manna. How awesome is that! Food appeared out of 'Nowhere.' Wouldn't you want to go back in time and be a part of the historical backdrop of the Bible to watch all these new experiences? How delighted we would be if we could see God in action. Is God still providing for His people? Does God continue to provide manna? Or is this manna story even real?

Recently, I was reading the story about the Israelites eating manna from the book of Exodus, and it dawned on me, I had seen God in action. I did! The thick, green leaves that carpeted the fences in my neighborhood, and the showers of shiny, green plant with the tiny neck, and an elongated body, those were food appearing from 'Nowhere.' That was God in action. I had a front seat to see God at work!

******

I have often heard people saying, "I never knew that I was poor." I'm thinking; they probably weren't poor. Poverty hurts, it smells, it shames. If you are poor, you will know it. You may not have the name for it, but you will know that your living situation is not good.

I was poor, and I knew it. I knew it because I felt it, I walked in its shame, I smelled it, and I saw it.

Hunger emptied my stomach then filled me up again until I was hungry no more. The cries of hungry children and babies filled the air and became a natural part of the rhythm in our community. I didn't hear the sweet sound of the birds as they danced in the high Jamaican winds, I didn't hear the beautiful sound of the evening breeze as it gently caressed the leaves. I heard the cries of hunger from young children – "me hungry, me hungry, me hungry." Children wept until weariness took over from hunger and rocked them to sleep.

Children who should be in school were out in the lane playing hop-scotch, jump rope, rounders, cricket. A hungry child cannot learn, and a teacher's passion for teaching is weak opponent when matched against hunger pangs. The few who could face down hunger pains didn't have the

Jehovah Jireh – God Provides

money to take the crowded taxi cabs to their place of learning.

Watching the lives of children in the ghetto, you could judge that if they have enough energy to play, they could go to school but playing protected them from thinking about their predicament. When they stopped playing hunger reared its ugly head.

I went to school without the long list of supplies that the school required and then spun stories to cover my shame. I remember the time I left the toilette paper roll on my beautiful, white dresser and my impeccable record of forgetting my jogging shoes every Wednesday.

Poverty smelled in the clothes sitting in wash tubs that waited for soap. Soap was the last priority in the constant line of needs to be filled. After a while, poverty ceased to smell, but it never stopped hurting.

******

Children are resilient, and we found ways to survive. During the summer, the boys went to the nearby bushes and picked naseberries and ackee. They sold what they could and took the remainder home to their families. The girls searched the almond trees for the dried fruit to make a sweet confectionary called almond drops. Still, in their hairy shells, we carefully cracked each shell with stones to reveal the tiny, sweet, brown, crunchy nut. We gathered the nuts, boiled them in sugar, then placed them on banana leaves to cool and harden. We walked around the neighborhood and adjoining streets and sold each piece for five cents. The process lasted an entire day, sometimes two. Each girl was rewarded with 50 cents or a dollar depending on how many whole almonds we were able to produce. I didn't do much almond breaking; I was heavy-handed, my almonds were pulverized, you couldn't tell the nuts from the shell. But I was good for something; I watched the girls as they cracked the nuts and made sure no one ate a single nut. I was also good at selling and was an expert at calculating the profits and sharing the money we made amongst the girls.

******

Our poverty was not driven by parents who were lazy. We were experiencing political turmoil in our country. Jobs and complete industries evaporated like cool mist in the desert. Hotels once buzzing with tourists now stood like ghosts, filling the vacuous arms of the major tourist towns. The few tourists who dared to visit our shores did not stay long enough for the hotels to employ workers for more than two or three days each week.

At the same time, there was a drought in our country; we didn't see a drop of rain for months, and the Government rationed water, locking off the pipes in low-income neighborhoods. The Parish Council (Local Government body) sent trucks one day each week to deliver water. By the time we fought our way to the truck the water was gone, and we went back home empty-handed.

There were times in our lives when it seems that man

Jehovah Jireh – God Provides

and God was against us.   Even the rain dismissed our existence, the rain clouds chose paths not covering our community, and it seems that God never heard the children's cries.

One night we went in search of water in one of the more affluent neighborhoods where water wasn't rationed. The night was a disaster. The owner of the house, a short white man with skinny legs and a rounded belly, was watering his garden when we approached him. He pulled his gun, pointed it at the group, and threatened to shoot. He called us the most degrading names: hooligans, vagabonds, dirty niggas, thieves. He didn't know us. There were people in our little group who worked in this community, cooked their meals, cleaned their homes, and cared for their children.

I guess he could not have understood our plight. How could he?   He was watering his flowers while we are looking for water to drink.

My father was in a rage, probably from shame that we were begging for a basic commodity, water, just plain water, and someone wanted to kill us because we were trying to live. Dada was ready to fight a gun-wielding man with his bare hands.   The other men restrained Dada. Sometimes the only thing a poor man has to show that he loves his children is his rage.   I was proud of Dada. Through his anger, I felt his love.

******

Jehovah Jireh – God Provides

God must have heard the cries of the children, "me hungry, me hungry" coming from our forgotten street because help came. Genesis 21verses 17-19 *"Then God heard the voice of the boy, and the angel of God called to Hagar from heaven, "What is wrong, Hagar? Do not be afraid, for God has heard the voice of the boy where he lies. Arise, lift up the boy and take him by the hand, for I will make him into a great nation." Then God opened her eyes, and she saw a well of water. So she went and filled the skin with water and gave the boy a drink...."*

I do not know from where it came but I know one day we woke up and realized that we had food from 'Nowhere.' Along the northwest side of our house, the fence was overflowing with thick green leaves. The leaves formed a straight line for about 200 feet into the other yards and carpeted the entire fence. We have never seen anything like this before. Mama and a few ladies said it looked like spinach. Out of wisdom or desperation, they picked the spinach and fed their families. At first, the taste was unpleasant, but gradually we developed an appetite for spinach. Every evening all the ladies and children would gather by the fence that separated our yards and picked what they needed for the evening's meal.

A few months after the spinach sprouted on our fences there was another provision, we called it porrell. There was a square of empty land behind our house and one day we saw some long, shiny green things growing on the fence. I found out later that porrell was a type of squash. I

Jehovah Jireh – God Provides

preferred porrell over spinach. Porrell had this hearty feeling to it and was firm and sweet. Porrell made the spinach tasted better. We picked baskets upon baskets of porrell. Our neighbors came with pots, baskets, or their kitchen towels to gather porrell.

The sounds of hunger left our community. God planted and watered the food we needed to survive. We ate vegetables not planted by the hands of man.

When we didn't need them, the spinach and the porrell disappeared.

******

Miracles come in several ways through people, the natural course of nature, through the animal kingdom. In the book of 1 Kings verse 17, God used a bird, to bring food to the prophet Elijah. *"And the word of the LORD came unto him, saying, ... I have commanded the ravens to feed thee there. So, he went and did according unto the word of the LORD... And the ravens brought him bread and flesh in the morning, and bread and flesh in the evening; and he drank of the brook. And it came to pass after a while, that the brook dried up.."*

God uses all aspects of His creation to provide for His people. Some we can explain easily, others not so much. Both the porrell and the spinach are seed-bearing plants. I believe God used birds to drop the seeds in our neighborhood just as he used the ravens to feed the prophet Elijah, 1 Kings 17 verses 2-6 - ...*and after the prophet told the king of the land that God would bring drought on the land God sent him away to hide by the river. Ravens fed him bread and meat in the morning, and meat in the evening.* In the middle of a drought, God planted vegetables and watered them with the mist of the morning dew to feed His people in Piggott Street.

******

All of creation is here to serve the Divine and to serve each other.
Nature reminds us that there is a Creator.

Jehovah Jireh – God Provides

11

The Unplanned Check
(Broken Promise)

And thou shalt take no gift: for the gift blinds the wise, and perverts the words of the righteous. Exodus 23 v 8.

The phone rang, and the familiar voice on the other end of the line made me an offer that was too good to refuse. I wanted what he had to offer; hard cold cash to provide food to feed my children and salvage my pride.

Was this an answer to my prayer or was this a test? I was desperate for the help being offered, but the tight nudge on my heart felt like the sound of a warning. Should I ignore the warning?

******

Raising children of my own was never a plan that resided within me. However, there were those rare moments when I saw a cute boy whom I secretly planned to marry, and I thought it would be nice to have some cute babies. It was in those idle dreams I vowed, my children would never go hungry. Never!

Fourteen years into raising my children, the picture I had painted – a pantry filled with grocery, a fridge

Jehovah Jireh – God Provides

brimming with fresh vegetables and fruits, and money to buy all the food we needed – was destroyed. The very thing I hated was becoming my reality.

******

Hunger is a cruel and dangerous human-made trap. The Devil is quite aware of the power that hunger possesses. Didn't the devil tempt Jesus with food? Hunger distorts the mind and has the power to corrupt the soul.

I had considered becoming a politician during my early teens. I believed having a position of political power I could put plans in place to ensure there was always food in Jamaica even in the worst political upheavals and even when there were disasters. My focus and one life goal - no child should know hunger.

******

Every promise has a cost. And I saw people who paid the high price, some with their lives. I've seen the shame on the faces of the men from my community as they unloaded the large bunches of bananas from their heads in the dark of the night. I heard their nervous laughter as they recounted how they barely escaped from the guards shooting at them. And I cannot forget Brother Jonas whose promise cost him his life.

Brother Jonas – A Promise Gone Wrong

It was June 26, 1983. The air was filled with hope and anticipation as thousands gathered to see the man of God. Buses, cars, and trucks filled with seekers came from all over Jamaica to see this man up close. Oral Roberts was

Jehovah Jireh – God Provides

the closest we were going to get to the power of God. And there he was on the stage, Oral Roberts! His presence seemed to fill the Park as his voice boomed through the massive black speakers. I cannot remember anything that he said but, I recalled the gunshots that made the call for sinners to step up to the altar and surrender to God seem more urgent.

As Oral Roberts made the call for sinners to surrender to God, the singers raised their voices, *"just as I am without one plea but as thy blood was shed for me and as thou bid me come to thee O lamb of God I come, I come."* Hundreds went up to the massive altar to receive their blessings. And in the middle of the altar call we heard, "POW, POW, POW, POW" and the altar call continued. Sinners met God, the sick got healed, and souls were saved. And somewhere outside the Park the price for a promise that would not materialize was paid.

Conversations started through the crowd of people about the shots we heard –

"Ole criminal get shot. Him trying to thief de stove from de high school."

"Me hear sey him ded. Police dem throw him inna dem car trunk and drive round till him breath lef him body."

The Friday before we went to see Oral Roberts, I had gone to pay Mama's partner money (community savings) to Miss Mary, our neighbor, the banker. Mr. Jonas, one of our church brothers, was in her yard washing pots. I heard him making plans to set up a stall at the upcoming reggae festival. He had already purchased the food, and now he needed a stove. He was filled with excitement, his pregnant wife would be delivering their baby soon and he had promised her that he would take care of everything and she shouldn't worry about.

When we got home from the Oral Roberts crusade, we were met with the sad news that our church brother, Mr. Jonas, was the one who was trying to steal the stove.

His baby was born on Monday June 27, 1983.

******

I never thought that providing food for my children could bring me to a moral crossroad. Making promises without knowing what it will take to deliver them is like walking a tightrope while wearing a blindfold. Without a firm moral code to guide us we could make choices with devastating results. We could be Brother Jonas.

A promise should be broken if it will break you. If satisfying a promise makes you compromise your values and takes your focus off the big picture, relinquish your hold on that promise. Break any promise that has short term pleasure and long-term pain.

******

Mark and I were successful in keeping my promise to put food on the table. Then came 2005, a few months after we moved to the USA and my life rebooted. We knew when we decided to migrate that there would be some challenges. However, the struggle to put food on the table

Jehovah Jireh – God Provides

wasn't one of the many problems we had envisioned.

When the children and I boarded the plane in Montego Bay Jamaica on August 19, 2004, at 3 PM, I had $200 cash to my name and no credit card. Seven hours later, I was in Maryland USA with zero dollars. All our money was used to transport us from the airport to the hotel. The introduction of what our life would be for the next 12 months was written on our first night in the USA; we lived from paycheck to paycheck.

I knew that life would get better. But before life gets better, we must deal with the bitter. How we deal with the bitter will determine the sweetness of our fruits.

I moved to the USA because I was offered my dream job. Mark followed us two months later only he never had a job and couldn't find work for a year. The first time in 14 years, we had a single income household and two homes to manage, we were still transitioning from Jamaica and had our home there to get ready for rental.

******

Mark's unemployment is one of the best gifts we received from God, yet we didn't know it at the time. While we were frantically searching for a job to provide for the children God was helping us to build a stable family in a new land.

Mark and I were worried about our financial needs, but God knows the emotional needs were far more important than the material things we couldn't afford. We were focused on giving our children what we didn't have, but

God created the space and time for us to teach our children the things we wished we had known. Today we have four well-adjusted young adults, only because they came home from school every day to their daddy who helped them to navigate the unpredictable changes in their lives and who helped them to build the foundation for living. I shuddered to think what our lives would have been today if God had given us what we wanted and not what we needed. Life has a way of giving us the things we need when we don't want to need them.

Romans 11 verses 33-34 says, *"O, the depth of the riches of the wisdom and knowledge of God! How unsearchable His judgments, and untraceable His ways! Who has known the mind of the Lord? Or who has been His counselor?"*

I now live in hindsight daily, instead of looking back five years from now to say "wow, God was doing a great thing" I look at my life every day, no matter how difficult and painful and say, "wow, God is working for good in my life." I may not know what the outcome will be, but I know it will be better than any plans I have for myself and my family.

******

The effects of our changing financial status were evident in the pantry and the fridge. One Sunday in 2005, I opened the pantry doors and was greeted by the bare shelves. I turned to the refrigerator, and the same sad message spilled out on me with the chilly air – 'You have

Jehovah Jireh – God Provides

failed your children. You should have never left Jamaica. You listened to your God and now He has abandoned you.'

I tried to push the negative thoughts aside but the truth was facing me, we had enough food to last the upcoming week and my next paycheck was two weeks away. We have a gap week, what would the children eat in the gap week?

The answer is in the Bible, Matthew 6 verses 25-27 Jesus said, *"Therefore I tell you, do not worry about your life, what you will eat or drink; or about your body, what you will wear. Is not life more than food, and the body more than clothes? Look at the birds of the air: They do not sow or reap or gather into barns— and yet your Heavenly Father feeds them. Are you not much more valuable than they? Who of you by worrying can add a single hour to his life?*

God makes promises to us. Bible scholars have stated that there are more than 7,000 promises that God has given to His people. Here are a few:

- *"He will never leave you nor forsake you."* Deuteronomy 31 verse 8.
- *"God will supply all your needs according to His riches in glory through Christ Jesus."* Philippians 4 verse 19.

******

My heart was painted with worry and I prayed earnestly to God to provide food for my children.

Jehovah Jireh – God Provides

There are two things you must know about me, I had a proclivity for helping God to accomplish my prayer requests, and I am frustratingly impatient. I drive my children and my husband crazy with my urgent demands. My timelines were most times unrealistic. Whenever I ask for something or for a task to be completed, I wanted it done yesterday. I had the same posture when I prayed to God. I want what I wanted when I want it.

It took me many years and several burning mistakes to rely on the promises of God and to let go of my pride and self-sufficiency.

*****

Monday, I searched through the Rolodex of my mind seeking someone I could call and ask for help. David's name came to mind, and as soon as I thought of David, the Divine said, **"No."** I knew no was the right answer. David had money, but I had a feeling his money was gained through nefarious activities. I tentatively dialed his number hoping he wouldn't answer, and that the call would go directly to voicemail. But it didn't.

"And thou shalt take no gift: for the gift blinds the wise, and perverts the words of the righteous." Exodus 23 v 8.

This verse from the Bible seems fitting for an ethics conference among auditing and accounting professionals. But as you ponder these 19 words, you will see these are truths good for the home and all of life's interactions.

Jehovah Jireh – God Provides

These 19 words are not just fit for professionals; they are beneficial for mothers, fathers, children, any member of society in all dealings. You see, gifts can put us in compromising positions – all have a price, there are no free gifts.

In high school, I read The Merchant of Venice by Shakespeare. Antonio criticized Shylock for the exorbitant fees he charged on loans. Shylock was an unscrupulous character, and everyone knew it. Later in the story, Antonio found himself in a situation where he needed money and needed it fast. So where did Antonio go? To unscrupulous Shylock. Instead of charging his usual heavy fees, Shylock went even further and told Antonio that if he didn't pay him back on time, Antonio would need to give him a pound of flesh. Antonio was desperate and agreed to the payment of his flesh.

How many of us have found ourselves in such a compromising situation? Sooner or later in your life, you will be faced with a moral decision. And you must ask and answer the question by yourself, do I sign the agreement and give up a pound of flesh? Should I take the gift and be perverted by the giver?

Would I give up a pound of flesh for food or would I watch my children suffer? I could also trust in God.

******

Unless you are safely grounded in the promises of God, you will be tempted to give up that pound of flesh.

Jehovah Jireh – God Provides

"Hello."

The familiar voice on the other side of the phone 4,000 miles away brought back cherished memories. We chatted about old times and then I made my first step onto the tight rope, blindfolded by my pride and a promise.

"I'm having a little problem and was wondering if I could borrow some money until I get my pay next week."

"How much do you need?"

My heart raced, my palms got sweaty. I had one foot on the tightrope, I knew danger was looming.

"Stop! Don't you believe in me?" A third person entered the conversation. It was the Divine.

"$200." I responded.

"No problem. I can get it to your bank account. Just give me your account information."

"I am God your Provider, trust in no other."

"Just one thing, yu will see more than what yu ask for, about five gran (US$5,000). When it gets to your account, call me and I will let yu know how to send it to me."

"No! I thought you were sending me the money? You cannot just give out my account number to other people."

I was throwing questions over the phone like a professional pitcher, but I was up against an even more professional batsman. You cannot make a deal with the devil on your terms. The devil calls the shots. The devil

Jehovah Jireh – God Provides

doesn't answer questions. Each response is a more glorious promise. He was smooth and relaxed; a snake doesn't make loud noises to catch its prey.

"No problem man. It is a simple transaction yu won't get into any trouble. Me and my brethren doing some business and we need a third party to send de money to me."

'You won't get into any trouble.' Whenever you hear that promise just run, do not think, run. I stepped off the tightrope and took off the blindfold.

"Hey. I am sorry to bother you. I will have to do without the loan."

"I will provide for you. I will supply your needs."

"No man, no worry bout dat me can still send you de $200."

"It is alright; I think I can manage. Thank you. Will call you some other time to catch up."

Click.

This loan doesn't pass the Brother Jonas test, this could cause me my reputation, my freedom, and my life.

******

And with the click of our phones, I realized the dangers of leaning on my understanding. So many lives have been destroyed because we cannot wait on God's promises.

I know that I could not sin against God, myself, and my family. How could I prove that I have a God who is the Great Provider when I went outside His will for food?

Jehovah Jireh – God Provides

Didn't Jesus admonish the devil about food? Matt 4 v 4, "But Jesus answered, *It is written: 'Man shall not live on bread alone, but on every word that comes from the mouth of God."*

The promise to my children was built on the foundation of raising them well. My commitment is to raise honest, loving, respectful, and responsible children. I went back to praying quietly in my mind, and I repented for my pride.

I waited on God.

******

I was resolute and firm that if God did not provide for me that week, I would break one of my promises to my children, they would be going to bed a few nights without food. I had six more days before we would run out of food.

Monday no answer.

Tuesday silence.

"God, where are you?"

Silence.

"Didn't you provide for the Israelites?" "I saw my mother asking for meat, and you provided now God I am standing in the gap for food to give my children."

Wednesday, I prayed, and no one came to save us.

Thursday, I prayed and still no answer, no still small voice, and no physical help. Only this time I started to sing unto God, a song of thanksgiving, this is my go-to song of worship.

"And He'll do it again; He'll do it again. Just take a

Jehovah Jireh – God Provides

look at where you are now and where you have been. He'll always come through for you. He is the same now as then. You may not know how, you may not know when, but He'll do it again." Shirley Caesar.

Friday morning nothing. God has been silent the entire week and the end is drawing near. Tomorrow is Saturday, and the pantry will be empty. We have butter, but the last slice of bread is gone. There is a handful of cereal, but no milk. We had rice and some potatoes, but no meat. What will the children eat for lunch and how will we buy gas for the car?

"God if you do not send us money I guess you will make what we have left in the pantry serve the entire week and you will find a way to get me to work."

Friday evening, I went home trusting that God will take care of our needs. Philippians 4 v 19 *My God will supply your needs according to the riches of his glory in Christ Jesus.* Mark picked me up from work, and we set on home to prepare the night's meal and put our four children to bed.

We checked the mailbox on our way in, a few bills, and a letter from my healthcare administrator. I haven't been to the doctor in a while, so I'm not concerned about this piece of mail. I opened the bills they are not due before the next pay cycle then I opened the health care mail.

The Psalmist David says, *"I was young, and now I am old, yet I have never seen the righteous forsaken or their*

Jehovah Jireh – God Provides

children begging bread. Psalm 37 v 25.

******

As I opened that last piece of mail, I was speechless, I could only hold its content up for Mark to see the miracle. There was God's answer, a check for $264.74, more than what the Devil wanted for my soul. The check was dated that very Monday, the day I tried helping God to provide for my children, the day I stepped on the tightrope and almost lost my way.

The check was a refund from my healthcare spending account. Every pay cycle I made payments towards foreseeable healthcare expenses, and whenever I visit the doctor, I would get a refund. There is this check in my hand, and I never went to the doctor or made a claim for a refund. I was later informed that I had overpaid into the account for eight months.

I know God is great and when God is all we have He will provide for us in His time. I have seen so many times when people around me are ruined because they could not rely on or wait on God's provision.

Is there a deadline that you have set for yourself to accomplish something or receive something? Have you waited patiently for that promotion and nothing happens? Isaiah 40 verse 31 tells us, *"they who wait for the Lord shall renew their strength."*

******

God will provide for all your needs.
Do not live by bread alone but on the promises of God.

Jehovah Jireh – God Provides

12

School Fee or the Spa?

"And you shall not glean your vineyard, nor shall you gather every grape of your vineyard; you shall leave them for the poor and the stranger: I am the Lord your God." Leviticus 19 verse 10

God had grander plans for the cash in my purse, all of it. $2,000 was all I wanted to spend, but the invisible hand restrained me, and I left the spa confused and disappointed.

I [used to] wish that God would show me the ending when He showed me the beginning, that would have made it so easy for me to obey. However, walking in faith is total trust in God without knowing what the outcome will be but having confidence that God's decision will be best for you and everyone involved. Faith is a complete surrender to the Divine.

******

Samuel was at the end of his proverbial rope desperate for a way out of his current situation. It was only noon, but every tick of the clock drove a nail in his heart and every hour that passed placed a wedge between him and his dreams – leaving the life of malignant poverty.

Jehovah Jireh – God Provides

Poverty was all Samuel knew; he lived from hand to mouth and walked precariously every day fearing entrapment into the gang life. If he ever lost sight of his dreams of going to college for just one minute, he would have slipped into the grave of gang leaders who were ready to snatch him up. They would school him on the ways of the street, a one-way ticket to hell that had snuffed out the lives of so many other young men before they saw the end of their teenage years.

The mere fact that Samuel finished high school was evidence of his grit and determination to break the chains that hold thousands captive in my community of Mt. Salem.

If you have never lived in extreme poverty you may not understand the control it has over the lives of its victims:

Poverty sinks deep into our brains, always reminding us that we belong only in despair.

Poverty modifies the structure of right and wrong with a sound rationale for every perverted action.

Poverty cautions us not to think too lofty and readily points out those who had dreamed and failed.

Poverty is the Pied Piper's flute charming its victim into dormancy.

Poverty shrinks our ability to see beyond each day, as it chokes the life out of any rational thinking.

Poverty tells us everyone is against us and an extended hand should never be trusted.

Jehovah Jireh – God Provides

Poverty reminds us that a five-year plan is a luxury only the rich can afford.

Poverty dangles crime before young men like free PhDs and most who accepted the admission never see post-adolescent.

The shortened life span propels young boys, who are just babies themselves to be baby daddies creating another round of poverty, another barrier so thick and high making it harder for the next generation to escape.

Samuel slipped through the cracks and demolished several of poverty's many chains; he finished high school, he lived pass his 18th birthday, and the gang leaders never schooled him. After leaving high school, he came to the sad realization that just having a high school diploma wasn't enough to get a decent paying job or to get into college, so he set out to break more chains.

He attended evening classes for 12 months and rushed home to complete his assignments; this would give him a shot to pass the national examinations. The work was hard, and the hours were long, but Samuel knew that sitting the exams and ultimately passing them would not only change the course of his life but that of his mother and two younger brothers. I know this not because I am intimate with all the details of his life but because I have been there myself. Passing a few subjects in the Caribbean Examination Council, (CXC) could mean a better paying job; moving from minimum wage to a position with more money and possibility of growth. Passing the exams would open the door to a college degree.

The only thing standing between him and a better life is 4,350 Jamaican dollars, and two more hours, two things that he could not control. Time was against him and his heart was burdened with this failure.

$4,350 was almost a month's wage for Samuel so you can understand why this was an impossible task for him to ask anyone for that kind of money.

Samuel knew that prayer works, but it seems as if God never heard his or was moving too slow. In church, we always hear, "God is always on time all the time." But when we are the ones waiting we throw God's schedule out the window.

******

One hundred and twenty miles away in another city I was budgeting the per diem I got for my business trip:

Per Diem	$7,350
Food	($1,500)
Taxi	($ 500)
Cash after business trip	**$4,350**
Spa	($2,000)
Balance to do whatever	**$2,350**

My company gave us per diem to cover three meals, but the money was ours to spend as we liked. Every trip provided extra cash that I would use to get a facial, buy face creams, and get my eyebrows waxed. My business trips were the only times when I could splurge on myself.

As soon as the training ended on Thursday, I took a

Jehovah Jireh – God Provides

cab from New Kingston and headed to the Jencare spa on Red Hills road. I have been looking forward to my visit to the spa since my trip was planned.

One hundred twenty miles from my home in Montego Bay, I had none of the guilt of proximity to prevent me from spending a fortune on myself, for $2,000 Jamaican I would be pampered. Nothing is wrong with that; after all, I could have spent it on food like my colleagues.

******

The spa smelled luxurious. All the women, the staff and those getting treatments sparkled like diamonds. The fluorescent light danced on their flawless skin. My trips to the spa made me feel like I was part of the small group of goddesses who could lavish on themselves. If only I could do this every month, I would sparkle like these women and wouldn't need makeup to cover my flaws. To be honest, I was paying for more than a treatment. I was paying to belong to a group that didn't even know that I existed.

I wrote my name in the appointment book and sat amongst the women with their perfect skin.

"You should leave; don't spend the cash." The small voice nudged at my heart.

"Why can't I spend my money on this one small treat? I barely ate for the past five days to treat myself." I reasoned.

"You should leave; don't spend the cash."

I grudgingly got up to erase my name from the Appointment. I returned to my seat to savor the

Jehovah Jireh – God Provides

atmosphere. The spotlights in the case holding the face creams and all the body scrubs, and lotions beckoned me.

I cannot come this far and not treat myself. I truly deserve to have my spa time. I went back and wrote my name in the appointment book.

"Listen to me; this is not yours to spend."

"This is my money. I could have eaten every cent at the fancy restaurants with my colleagues. I can do whatever I want."

My money. How silly was I? Nothing belongs to me. Everything I am and own belongs to the Creator. *"The earth is the Lord's and all that is in it.* Psalm 24 verse 1."

So much of the world's suffering comes from our miseducation of who owns the world's assets. We own nothing. Everything we have is borrowed, and we should not hold them too tightly.

I didn't want to leave without getting my treatments. But the nagging feeling in my heart told me it was wrong to spend the money. I entered my name in the book and erased it again and repeated this for four more times until the receptionist told me to make up my mind as she was closing the appointments, the spa was closing in an hour.

Eventually, I picked up my purse and left without my facial or my products, and my eyebrows were the same as when I left home. I felt stupid walking out of the spa without getting anything; I did not spend a dollar. I could have done my eyebrows, that was only $100. I wondered

Jehovah Jireh – God Provides

what those women were thinking about me, "silly girl can't afford spa treatment and trying to fake it." The truth is, they were not thinking about me.

******

Friday morning, I had forgotten about my foiled attempt to treat myself last evening and was excited to get home to my family. The tiny plane bounced on the clouds and kept all six passengers holding on to their seatbelts for the entire flight. The pilot landed the plane safely, and I took a cab to my office. Around noon I got to my office picked up the phone and called Mark to let him know I was back in town.

Mark didn't pick up, Samuel did.

Someone recently asked me, what the difference between a miracle and luck? Luck is opportunity meeting preparation. However, a miracle for me is when you do not have the answers, when you do not have the strength, and when there are no resources, and no opportunities but a problem is resolved, a bill is paid, sicknesses are destroyed, food shows up, and in Samuel's case, his entire exam fees are paid without him asking for help.

'Hello, Samuel speaking, Mr. Kameka's office", Samuel's soft voice glided through the phone.

"Hi Samuel, how are you, where is Mark?"

"He just stepped out, he will return shortly."

"Who should I say is calling?"

"Tell him Michelle called."

There was something about Samuel's voice that seems

void of joy. What I heard on my side of the phone was someone in need of help. I hesitated to ask him if something was wrong. I know Samuel, but we weren't close friends, and I didn't want to seem intrusive. I was about to hang up the phone, but instead, the words slipped from my lips without my permission.

"Samuel, is something wrong? You do not sound right."

No sooner had I asked the question, Samuel unburdened the load he was carrying all morning and the distress that he wore all his life. In less than five minutes I learned more about Samuel than I had in the ten years I have seen him in church. He told me he had two hours to pay $4,350 or he would have to spend another year going to evening classes, find money for that registration and wait another year to do the exams.

It was only then it clicked, it all came together $4,350 is all the cash I had in my purse. Life is not always about my wants and this time it was about Samuel and his exam fees.

"Samuel it is going to be ok, I will ask Mark to give you a check."

I couldn't leave work to get the cash to him on time. I didn't have the money in the bank, but I would deposit the cash first thing on Monday morning before the check cleared. There was silence on the other end of the line, then he asked;

"Michelle, which Michelle is this?"

Jehovah Jireh – God Provides

Some people know me as Gwen others Michelle.

"Michelle Kameka."

"Ahh, oh man. Mrs. Kameka if I knew it was you I wouldn't have told you so much."

Samuel thought he was sharing his story with a friend who shared my name.

These four words, 'if I had known,' are usually echoes from the wounds of our thoughtless actions or simple mistakes. God will use our 'if I had knowns' to bless us. Whenever a miracle is about to materialize, your 'if I had knowns' will not matter.

"Samuel, it is going to be alright. Don't you see that this is God's provision?"

I told him how I got the money and how I couldn't spend it. It was then that he broke the barrier of pride and accepted the gift from God. Not from me but God. Twenty hours before, I didn't know about his problem, but God knew and provided for him. I didn't need to see the ending I am only required to obey.

Samuel passed his exams and is now living a life beyond amazing. A year later I too got a similar gift, except it was much more significant. God saw my obedience and blessed me immensely. I didn't tie my blessings with the gift I made to Samuel until I was piecing all the miracles of my life together.

Jehovah Jireh – God Provides

"Kindness to the poor is a loan to the LORD, and He will repay the lender." Proverbs 19 verse 17. I must add, God repays with interest.

******

God is always on time.

Jehovah Jireh – God Provides

13

A Job Beyond Amazing

"This is what the LORD says: 'Dig this valley full of ditches.'... For the LORD says, 'You will not see wind or rain, but the valley will be filled with water, and you will drink—you and your cattle and your animals.'... This is a simple matter in the sight of the LORD.... The next morning, at the time of the morning sacrifice, water suddenly flowed from the direction of Edom and filled the land.... 2 Kings 3 verses 15-20

I know I must take the leap of faith; there was no other way. My heart raced like wildfire consuming the vast Kalahari Desert. With eyes wide open, I looked out in the horizon of my life, and there was no safety net, except the voice of God promising to take care of me. If the voice that told me to resign my job wasn't the voice of God I would be crushed.

I resigned my job!

******

Eight years out of college I had a decent job, but I was still in the financial trenches. Being the only family member to have graduated high school and then college obfuscated my family's idea of my financial obligations to them and how much money I was earning. The monthly emergencies from my extended family waited on my paychecks like a merciless bill collector. I was hopelessly indebted to everyone who cheered me on as I walked out of the ghetto and I didn't know how to set up boundaries.

******

I was the senior accountant at Delight.Com. God provided this job after I had my son and needed to reduce my travel time. I called Delight.Com my launching pad into faith, but that would be four years after my adventuresome journey to the interview.

The phone call for the accounting position at Delight.Com came on a Wednesday evening, and I had to be at the interview the next morning at 10 o'clock. I didn't have a suit that I thought was appropriate for the meeting.

Early Thursday morning Mark and I sat in our 1962 VW bug and waited for the clothing store to open. As soon as the store was opened, we rushed in, and I bought a skirt suit made with olive colored linen fabric. That was the only time in my life that I have entered a store and only looked at what I was going to buy. We dashed into the VW, and while Mark was driving at top speed, I was changing into my new suit. I had no clue that what we accomplished that day was even possible. We got to the interview on time, and I got the job.

******

I wanted more for myself, my three-year diploma from

Jehovah Jireh – God Provides

the College of Arts Science and Technology was dwarfed by the development of the country and the prized bachelor's degree that was now being offered by my alma mater. I had to take the next step and earn my bachelor's degree if I wanted to progress my career.

During a training session hosted by our parent company, I overheard a young man telling his friends about the classes he attended on weekends at a university named Nova. That conversation changed the trajectory of my life. Before that chance conversation, I thought that the only way to get further education was going back to college fulltime, a path I could not afford financially or emotionally.

I returned from the training with a plan to learn more about this Nova University. It was only then that my gaze rested on the CEO's degrees and I noticed that he too went to Nova, imagine that. It is funny that you cannot find an item of worth until you start looking for that specific thing. For almost four years I had visited the CEO's office to get payment vouchers approved, letters signed, and to discuss monthly financial reports but I never saw his degree from Nova South Eastern University on the wall behind his desk. How could that be? I must have been in that office more than a thousand times, and my eyes never traveled to the degrees in their glass frames, placed prominently in his office.

His diploma said it was issued in Florida, it might not be the same university. I put courage on during one of my visits to get the CEO to sign a batch of documents and asked,

"Mr. Snow, did you attend college in Florida?"

"Oh.   No. Nova has classes in Ocho Rios on the weekends."

Ocho Rios is approximately sixty miles from where I lived. I could do that. I thought to myself. I braced myself with more courage....

"Mr. Snow, do you have the number for the school? I want to register."

"I don't have any information for the school. "You will have to search the phone book."

It was back before the internet had a link for everything and business numbers were kept in Rolodexes, a plastic container with paper inserts on which names, telephone numbers, and addresses were written in alphabetical order.

I was disappointed. However, I knew that I would get this information without his help. I approached his secretary to retrieve the hidden piece of the puzzle that would unlock the doors to my future.

"Denise, could you check Mr. Snow 's Rolodex to see if he has the contact information for Nova University?"

I asked in a matter of fact way and may have given her the impression that this was an approved request. She flipped through the cards in the plastic container holding all of Mr. Snow's business contacts and just like that, right under N, there was Nova South Eastern University, the

Jehovah Jireh – God Provides

telephone number, and the administrator's name, Mr. Rose.

I called up Mr. Rose that very day and registered to start college the next semester, October 1996. I shared my great find with all the ladies in the office, including Denise, all of whom only had a three-year diploma. Soon the entire office would earn either their bachelor's or master's degree from Nova South Eastern and a few of us even got both degrees from the university.

******

I never thought this college thing out straight; how was I going to pay the tuition?   Delight.Com approved a scholarship that paid 11,000 Jamaican Dollars after I passed each semester but would leave me with a debt of J$44,000 every semester and I had no way of paying the first dollar. I had J$265,000 worth of reasons not to sign up for college, that is what it would cost me for the 18 months, but I could not resist this challenge, and I prayed to God for a way out.

Mr. Rose also had hope that I was going to pay for my tuition. I wondered if he knew my financial situation if he would have admitted me in the program. For five months, October 1996 to February 1997, Mr. Rose would ask,

"Ms. Gwen, when are you going to pay your tuition?"

"Next week sir."

Only next week never came, well, except for the January of 1997 when I paid the $11, 000 that Delight.Com paid for the first semester. Mr. Rose never gave up asking, and I never gave up hope and faith in God. The Bible says,

Jehovah Jireh – God Provides

"faith is the substance of things hoped for, the evidence of things not seen," Hebrews 11 verse 1. God had taken me through three years of college before surely God can deliver me again.

******

Have you ever felt the moment when the tides of your situation changed? For me, it was January 1997, I cannot recall the date, but it was in the afternoon, about 3'oclock. I went to the lunch room for water, and I saw the company's driver, Mr. Whitaker. I sat with him, and we talked about the goodness of God and the difficulty of raising children on a meager salary. Mr. Whitaker was in the thick of raising five teenagers, and like me, he had challenges that he pushed through every day. I shared with him how God took me through some challenging times. I was cautious in saying the name of Jesus because I wanted to respect his religion. He is a Jehovah's witness and only spoke of God or Jehovah.

While we were talking, I felt a sudden shift in my life. I had to stop and share with Mr. Whitaker the change that I felt in my mind and spirit. I didn't hear or see anything in the physical, but for a moment I felt that my life was going to move in a new direction. If I should try and explain this shift – it felt like a brief movie clip of my life flashed before my mind's eyes. I saw myself as little girl in a meadow filled with Daffodils and Spanish Needles. The scene stretched out before me and everything around me was filled with light and warmth. The little girl seemed

Jehovah Jireh – God Provides

happy and content and I could hear the Divine saying –

"That little girl is you I will take care of you."

This all happened in a split second.

"Mr. Whitaker, Jesus is going to do something great in my life, and I believe it."

The words spilled from my mouth before my mind could rearrange them to match Mr. Whitaker's religion. Why would I say something like that in the middle of consoling someone? First, I mentioned the name of Jesus, and second, I was talking about my life and not his being changed. He never questioned the authenticity of what I declared, but he asked –

"Gwen, why couldn't you say Jehovah?"

We can be so blinded by religion that we miss seeing God. For the first time, I had to declare to Mr. Whitaker that Jesus is Lord and we must serve him. We chatted for a few more minutes, and I went back to work

******

"You must resign, and I will take care of you."

The words startled me. I heard the words echoed inside me as I was getting ready to clear my desk for the evening. I didn't hear this voice with my ears; this voice was on my inside. I knew this was the voice of God. It was not an ask; it was a command.

Who does that? Just up and leave a job because the Divine told them to. Well, Abraham did, but I am no Abraham, and I do not want to lead a nation. All I wanted from God was an increase in my pay at Delight.Com so that

Jehovah Jireh – God Provides

I could pay my tuition and take care of my family.

God's plans for our lives are much more significant, more satisfying, more colorful, more impactful than anything we can plan for ourselves. It is like our plans for our children except more magnificent; while our children are satisfied just going to elementary school you and I are ten years ahead planning high school and college and even their career.

I knew the miracles that I wanted. I thought I knew what was best for me and didn't need God's input on the planning. I already had the plan, and God needed to do the work. I had it all twisted. We live the abundant life when we work according to God's blueprint for our lives. God is not a miracle ATM, He is the Divine Creator of all and He knows the ending when He created the beginning.

"God, I know you make the universe, you put the stars into place, you have taken me through challenging times, but I cannot leave my job."

"You must resign, and I will take care of you."

"God, can't you see that I have two children to feed, how can I leave my job? God, you are asking too much from me. My faith is not that big."

God was eager to bless me, and His words kept echoing in my heart –

"Resign, and I will take care of you. Trust in me."

I was resolute. I could not put so much trust in God; I will not leave my job. We do not have because we do not trust the Giver. The miracle of receiving takes courage and

Jehovah Jireh – God Provides

trust. God would not stop speaking this promise to me and I had to call on someone who knew God better than me, I called my Mama. Through tears, I shared with her.

"Mama, God is telling me to leave my job, and He will take care of me. How will I take care of the children? How will we manage? And if I just get up and leave my job people will think that I am crazy."

Mama listened, as wise people do and then in wisdom responded –

"Me dawta, yu know the voice of God, don't you?"

"Yes, Mama."

"Well, you don't have a choice you have to obey the voice of God. If you don't trust Him and obey Him, you can't get what Him have fi you."

"Yes, Mama."

"And memba fi stop worry bout wha people tink bout you"

"Yes, Mama."

******

I failed the test! I could not resign, and January rolled into February. When we do not obey the voice of God, we entangle ourselves in the web of confusion that requires another miracle.

I decided to help God to create this miracle, and so I asked my friends to help me find a job. One friend got me an interview with Tropical, a company that made aluminum windows and doors. That friend would prove to be a source of destruction later in my life. My trying to help

Jehovah Jireh – God Provides

myself put me in a precarious position, I started a relationship that could have cost me everything.

A job with Tropical could be the answer to my prayers. The office was only a minute walk from where I worked. The interview went well – I was offered the job on the spot, and a twenty percent increase above my current pay. The young lady who conducted the interview told me that I would get the offer letter on Monday morning. I was overjoyed.

God told me to resign. He never told me to search for a job. I did it my way, and it paid off. No, it didn't.

If I accepted Tropical's offer my financial situation wouldn't change; I would have a new boss and my old worries. I consoled myself at least it is a change of pace.

I wasted no time, I went directly to Human Resources director, Mrs. Lewis, and told her that I just did an interview and that Tropical made me a verbal offer. I also offered a verbal resignation. Mrs. Lewis cautioned me -

"Gwen, you should never resign until you get an offer letter and I cannot announce your resignation until you give me a formal letter."

Mrs. Lewis didn't know that I was in a rush to partially obey God. Look at me trying to outsmart God. In my mind, if I sent in the resignation letter before I got the formal offer I was still following the Divine. O what lies we tell ourselves when we are living outside the banner of God's love and instructions. I went to my desk and quickly typed the resignation letter and sent it to Mrs.

Lewis.

******

And now, I am standing on the ledge with eyes wide open looking out at the horizon of my life. I had known many situations where the deal fell through before ink touched the paper. What have I done? I was free falling, tumbling, grazing through thin air.

Fifteen minutes later the phone rang and just before I got crushed God delivered on His promise.

"Hello, is this Gwen?" The voice was unfamiliar.

"Yes, this is Gwen" I answered tentatively.

The woman on the other end of the phone continued,

"My name is Dianne Polle, you do not know me, but the auditors always talked about you and the quality of your work. They only had good things to say about you. I used to be the Audit Director (external auditor) for your company. I am at Crepe, and we have two positions to fill and would like you to come in for an interview. Are you interested?"

"Yes."

I gave her an emphatic yes. I wasn't just saying yes to an interview I was saying yes to God's divine plan for me. My resignation, my acceptance of Mrs. Polle's offer to an interview opened my eyes to see a glimpse of the Divine's perfect plan for my life. I was amazed by the deep certainty I felt that my life would change for the better and I felt peace for the first time in a long time about my future.

God is always fighting for us to live the abundant life,

Jehovah Jireh – God Provides

but we have made ourselves into our little gods, and we live by our own rules. In the book of Matthew Jesus said, *"come unto me, all ye that labor and are heavy laden, and I will give you rest. Take my yoke upon you and learn of me; for I am meek and lowly in heart: and ye shall find rest unto your souls."* Matt 11 verses 28-29.

I didn't know how to take on the full yoke of Christ successfully, but thankfully Christ pursued me against my best judgment.

I was now tied up in my own safety net, tied up and incompetent to undo the troubles that I have caused myself. What if the letter comes from Tropical on Monday, what would I tell them? I called Mark and told him my worries, and he assured me that I would make the right decision and should not worry about Monday. Isn't that what Jesus said in Matthew 6 verse 34? *"Therefore, do not worry about tomorrow, for tomorrow will worry about itself. Today has enough trouble of its own."*

Monday came and with it the letter from Tropical, they wanted an answer that same day. My interview with Crepe was Thursday. I called Tropical ….. and with eyes wide opened, I jumped off the ledge into God's mercy.

I told Human Resources that I could not accept the job. I was honest and told about the interview with Crepe.

I jumped…God, please catch me!

******

Thursday morning Mark dropped me off at the headquarters. I was nervous as a squirrel who slept through

Jehovah Jireh – God Provides

summer. I did not know much about Crepe, and I wasn't quite prepared to answer many questions about the company.

I met the Chief Financial Officer for my interview, Mr. Peter Cummings. Mr. Cummings, a middle-aged English man wearing a blue, short-sleeved shirt and a red tie. He was pleasant and very polite. He asked me a few questions about my work experience, and he told me about the open positions. Crepe needed a Group Internal Auditor based in HQ and a Cost Controller for one of the hotels.

I had set my mind on the cost controller position and was excited to share with Mr. Cummings the skills that I had that would make me the best candidate for that job. I am not sure if he heard my selling points because he too had already made up his mind what position I was skilled to perform.

"I think you will make a great auditor."

Mr. Cummings was laying the foundation of my life for the next twenty years; I wish he knew he was part of a more excellent plan. He offered me the job on the spot and guess what? My new salary plus a bonus was more than a 100% increase over my old salary. He went on to tell me about the benefits that would include scholarships to complete bachelor's and master's degree to study at the one and only Nova South Eastern University. It doesn't stop there, Mr. Cummings asked if there is anything else that he could do for me, and I do not know how or why I told him that I owed Nova 44,000 Jamaican dollars or USD$1,276.

Jehovah Jireh – God Provides

I could not believe it when he said he would pay the outstanding balance if I could join the company in two weeks.   I had already given in my resignation and was ready to start in the next two weeks.

******

Our life is like a puzzle except we do not have the box with the complete picture to put the pieces together.   And we do not need the final image because we are not responsible for setting the bits of our lives together.   Our job is to listen to and obey the voice of God.

Like the three kings in the book of 2 Kings, our job is to dig the ditches and wait on the Divine to provide the water, even in the desert where there is no rain.

******

With God all things are possible.
Dig ditches; God will fill them.

Jehovah Jireh – God Provides

God is Our Lord

Jehovah-Rohi

"...I urge you to live a life worthy of the calling you have received. Be completely humble and gentle; be patient, bearing with one another in love. There is one body and one Spirit, just as you were called to one hope when you were called; one Lord, one faith, one baptism; one God and Father of all, who is over all and through all and in all." **Ephesians 4 verses 1-6.**

14

Multiplication

"Give, and it will be given to you. They will pour into your lap a good measure-- pressed down, shaken together, and running over. For by your standard of measure it will be measured to you in return." Luke 6 v 38

Lisa was her name. She is the young lady who taught me the miracle principle of multiplication - when we share our gifts with others, the Divine will bless us more than we had given away. It is like this, a farmer has a pumpkin seed, he can choose to eat it now and be satisfied, or he can plant the seed, and after 100 days he can reap 12 pumpkins with approximately 1,200 seeds.

No, she didn't give me that analogy, but as I watched my husband reaping pumpkins from his garden in the summer of 2017, I was taken back to my interaction with Lisa ten years before, in July of 2007.

My company sent me to represent the organization at the Black MBA conference held in Orlando, Florida. The meeting provided training sessions covering a variety of topics and was a melting pot for innovative ideas to help Black professionals succeed as leaders and entrepreneurs. 2007 was the Black MBA's 29th anniversary, and the conference theme was 'Relevance - how to stay 'Current and Credible.'

That's a question we should all ask ourselves – how do we stay relevant in a changing world and maintain credibility at the same time? I sat in many sessions for three days. I learned about supporting Black businesses and how to save money for the future. The speakers were experts, and knowledgeable, but none of them answered the question, 'how do I stay relevant and credible at the same time?'

Throughout your lifetime you will find that your greatest teachers are ordinary people whom you thought had little to offer. The greatest lessons have no curriculum; they come to you through human interacting with hearts wide open. Be open to learn wherever you are, be ready to listen to life's teachers, whoever they are, and be quick to apply the lessons you learn – it is in the application that real learning takes place.

******

On the final night of the conference, there was a banquet. We were served a five-course meal, and there would be dancing to celebrate the successful event. In my rush to get to the banquet, I left my glasses in my hotel room. My lack of sight and the diminished lighting in the banquet hall restrained my ability to find the table where all my colleagues were seated.

The tables were filling up. I spotted a table at the back of the room with an empty chair and quietly slid in beside the group already chatting excitedly amongst themselves. I

Jehovah Rohi – God is Our Lord

learned that my table mates were college students from New York who came to the conference with their professor. The college had a program that provided students exposure to leaders who have made a name for themselves. I introduced myself and laughingly shared the story of how I'd ended up at their table.

I had taken the last chair, the chair belonging to Lisa. Lisa arrived about 15 minutes after I had settled into her space.

"Hello, you are sitting in my seat." She smiled as she spoke. Her eyes shone through the darkness.

"I am so sorry to have taken your chair." I hurriedly pushed away from the table getting ready to leave.

"No worries." Lisa turned around and found an idle chair pushed up against the wall.

She pulled the chair to the table and sat to my left. Lisa seemed self-assured, she was well dressed, and she looked happy - a warm smile covered her face. Everything looks better in the dark.

"Hi, my name is Gwen, and I'm from Maryland."

"I'm Lisa. I live in New York."

"You have an accent." "Where are you from?"

"Jamaica."

"Me too."

We chatted about our Jamaican culture, exchanged notes about our transition to the USA, and I told her about my children. We had so much in common; she also had children, two girls, and a boy. She was effervescent and

Jehovah Rohi – God is Our Lord

pleasant. Life is perfect when we do not unravel matters of the heart.

I noticed that while the other girls were chatting with each other, they never included Lisa in their conversations. As I looked closer at the scene around the table, I could see, that life had knocked her down a few times. She could have been me. Lisa reflects my past, a mirror of my days in high school and college; the scars of hardships were hidden in the dim light.

******

"Ask her if she knows Jesus."

"Lord you know I had no plans to discuss anything heavy tonight."

God doesn't work in our time and convenience. God doesn't stop caring for you because you are filled with drugs laying in the gutters, in prison heading to death row, a prostitute laying in an unfamiliar bed, or at a banquet eating a five-course meal. God is everywhere, always seeking and searching for us.

"Lisa, do you know Jesus?"

"Yes, my grandmother brought us up in the church. I had to pray to God this morning; I just had to."

Frustration boiled in her voice replacing the effervescent smile. I wanted to ask her what she prayed about but thought that was too pushy.

"Tell her about your hardships in college. Tell her how I provided for you."

"Ok, Lord."

Jehovah Rohi – God is Our Lord

"Lisa, I grew up in an impoverished family and never knew that college was a possibility…I had no clue how my life would turn out even after I got out of college and look at what God has done for me."

I told Lisa everything about my college experience and how my Auntie C treated me. I shared how God used an unpleasant situation to make my life better. The darkness made it easy to share my personal stories. Lisa held on to my hand and started to sob.

"Thank you! Thank you! Thank you! How did you know that I needed to hear this? I had given up hope. This morning when I told my children that I loved them, I was telling them goodbye."

"Goodbye?" "Why?"

Lisa asked me to look at her suit. The pants she was wearing was a size too small and was barely holding on by a few threads and some safety pins. We must come up close to our neighbors or understand their sorrows and pain. We must look so that we can see.

"Gwen, my life is hard. I have been wearing this suit for the entire conference, for all five days. Every night I wash my blouse and put new stitches in my jacket and pants. Gwen, I'm only here because another student got ill after she paid for the conference and she couldn't get a refund. I can't afford this."

She spread her arms emphatically, highlighting the splendor of the room in comparison to her drab clothing. Lisa continued to pour her heart out –

Jehovah Rohi – God is Our Lord

"The other students changed their clothes every day. They have money to buy food; I can only eat whenever we have group meals."

Lisa had a hard life; only now her hardships were multiplied when she compared her life to the 'opulence' of the other students and the pomp and pageantry of the event. Comparing your life to others can steal your joy if it is not contained within truth and love. We are not blind, so we will see the material gains that others have. However, when we know who our God is, we can see the abundance in another's life and celebrate with them knowing our day of reaping will come. Lisa's heart was wandering because of the lies she heard before and believed.

Lies tell us - "You will never amount to anything." "You don't belong." "This good thing is by chance; it will never happen to you again."

Truth tells us – "Your hardships will not kill you." "You will get through this." "You are created for greatness." "You have a right to be here."

******

God had orchestrated this moment, all the details: the sick classmate, my forgotten glasses, me taking her chair, every step was a setup by God to work a miracle in our lives.

"Lisa, God will take care of you. You are going to be fine."

I went on to tell her other stories of God's hand in my life. We exchanged phone numbers, and I left feeling great that I had encouraged someone. But that wasn't the only plan God had for our meeting. That night as I got ready for bed I felt the need to write Lisa a check for US$500. I argued with God –

"God, you don't expect me to give a check for that amount to a stranger! God, I have committed to the children in Jamaica to buy their books for school, that's US$2,500 that I am already struggling to find and to add another US$500…God, don't you think you are asking too much of me?"

In the book of James 2 verse 15-16, James said – *"Suppose a brother or sister is without clothes and daily food. If one of you tells him, "Go in peace; stay warm and well fed," but does not provide for his physical needs, what good is that?*

Lisa wasn't a stranger; she is my sister. I was leaving the conference without learning the lesson. This is a lesson that continuously shows up in my life. God will keep repeating the curriculum until the student passes the test. My lessons to learn: everyone is my brother and my sister, and I am not the ultimate decision maker of who should receive what God has placed under my guardianship. What is the lesson that you need to learn?

If I didn't provide for Lisa, my faith wasn't relevant and lacked credibility. How could I justify my love for God and not help a sister in need? The reliability of our faith is in our love for our brothers and sisters, and our love is seen in how we help those in need. Admittedly, I was

Jehovah Rohi – God is Our Lord

struggling to find US$2,500 to buy books for the children in Jamaica, but I could afford US$500.

******

The next day was the check-out day. Lisa was on my mind, the conversation we had last night, and what God told me to do. I picked up the phone a few times but refused to call her. As I entered the hotel's lobby, I bumped into Lisa. She was so happy to see me and thanked me for the encouragement. I watched as she walked towards the exit. She was about 50 feet away when my conscience called out to me, and I called her back. I quickly wrote a check for US$350, folded it, and handed it to her. Lisa put the check away without looking at it and then ask if she could pray for me. Lisa prayed that God would bless my gift to her ten times.

That very weekend I got a call from a friend in Jamaica telling me that she will pay for all the books the children needed, US$2,500. I didn't give the US$500, but God used the opportunity to teach me to trust Him and to strengthen my shaky faith.

"But whoever has the world's goods, and sees his brother in need and closes his heart against him, how does the love of God abide in him?" John 3 v 17

Many Christians quote Luke 6 verse 38, but they leave out "Give, and it will be given to you." We are so self-centered and foolish believing God will forget His own words. The pouring, press down, shaken together, and the running over will not take place until we have completed the act of giving to those in need.

"Give, and it will be given to you. They will pour into your lap a good measure-- pressed down, shaken together, and running over. For by your standard of measure it will be measured to you in return." Luke 6 v 38

******

Money that we give to the poor multiplies.
Miracles happen when we speak with hearts wide open.
Envy distorts the plan God has for your life.
Our relevance and credibility come from extending kindness to another.

Jehovah Rohi – God is Our Lord

15

Open Your Hands Wide

"And he said to him, "You shall love the Lord your God with all your heart and with all your soul and with all your mind. This is the great and first commandment. And a second is like it: You shall love your neighbor as yourself." Matthew 22:37-3

"Get up and read my words."
I was tired, and jet lagged. I pulled the covers over my shoulders and closed my eyes tightly. I wanted to sleep.
"Get up and read my words."
"No. I will read the Bible tomorrow."
When God wants to teach you a lesson, He doesn't choose a time that is convenient for you. God doesn't wear a watch, and He is not restricted by time. In God's domain, the school is always open, and it is up to the student to show up and learn.

******

February 25, 2013, I was 6,000 miles away from home in Baku Azerbaijan. At 3 AM I heard the voice of God calling me to read the Bible. I had done wrong in His sight, and like a good Father, God came to teach me the right thing. God came to correct my faulty thinking.

Jehovah Rohi – God is Our Lord

I placed the pillow over my head, dug my hands deeper into the covers, and pulled my knees closer to my chest. I could read the Bible tomorrow morning.

"Get up and read my word."

That wasn't a question; it was a firm command. There was something about the call; it sounded like Mama calling me after I did something wrong.

I got up, opened the hotel's Bible, and I saw an unfamiliar scripture, delivering a familiar request from God. A command of giving and blessing written in a way that brought new meaning to sharing with others. Before that morning in Azerbaijan I only gave to people I saw worthy, people I thought never squandered their opportunities, and people I thought were hardworking. The words on the pages made me forget my jetlag and sleepiness, and I sat upright and read –

"You shall generously give to him, and your heart shall not be grieved when you give to him, because for this thing the LORD your God will bless you in all your work and in all your undertakings. For the poor will never cease to be in the land; therefore, I command you, saying, 'You shall freely open your hand to your brother, to your needy and poor in your land." Deuteronomy 15 verses 10 and 11

******

Wow…immediately I knew what God was telling me. God did not leave any room for interpretation – "Give to him…... open your hand to your brother."

The day before, my brother-in-law, Patrick, wanted

Jehovah Rohi – God is Our Lord

money to buy a cow. Mark and I discussed the matter, and I was adamant that he should repay us to instill some discipline. I know my mandate is to give with love. I was out of my league requesting repayment, trying to teach discipline. I had slipped back into an old habit, playing 'god'.

God never placed it on my heart to instill discipline in anyone; I was called to love and give with grace. The same grace with which God has blessed me.

I was immediately convicted by the word of God, and I repented. What if God had dealt with me in the same manner that I was planning to treat my brother-in-law? I would forever be in debt. I called Mark and shared with him the lesson that I had learned, and I apologized for the terrible words I spoke earlier.

How could my husband see the love of God if I was not showing compassion and kindness to others?

God saw my heart and it wasn't in a good condition. The heart must be surrendered daily to the Divine. Now, one of my daily prayers, before I open my eyes in the morning, is from Psalm 139 – *"Search me O God and know my heart: try me and know my thoughts: And see if there be any wicked in me, cleanse me and set me free."*

******

To be used by God is to be available to go to places you had no plans of going. It is to serve people who cannot give back to you. To serve God, we must live spontaneously and outrageously on the edge of life: loving

Jehovah Rohi – God is Our Lord

and helping the poor, listening to the lonely, and seeking the lost, and giving massively of our material possessions and our time without expectations.

You might be saying; I've never heard from God? But have you made yourself available to hear from God? God pursues all of us to teach us His ways and to use us to accomplish His plans, not because we are good or perfect but because He loves us with an everlasting love.

We are His precious gems, and His pursuit of us is to refine us and to give us the abundant life. We do not hear the voice of God because we are so busy scheming and planning. We are happy in our sinful condition, and we do not want to change our ways, we are afraid to surrender all to the Divine.

Psalm 46 tells us, *"be still and know that I am God..."* We must be still and quiet to hear the voice of God. It is no wonder that our greatest ideas come to us in our dreams or when we are showering, times when we are not scheming and dealing.

******

What struggles do you have that you drag around with you like a ball and chain? If God can wake me up at 3 AM. to buy my brother-in-law a cow, and to correct my stinking thinking, imagine what He can do for you.

Some miracles happen for you, and there are others where you are the conduit for the miracle to take place. Be prepared in both situations.

Jesus said, *"If you love me, you will keep my*

Jehovah Rohi – God is Our Lord

commandments." What are those commandments? *Jesus answered by saying, "Love the Lord your God with all your heart, with all your soul, and with all your mind. This is the greatest and most important commandment." The second is: "Love your neighbor as yourself."* John 15:14 and Matthew 22:34–36

******

Love your neighbor as yourself.
Be still and hear the voice of God.
Open your hands wide and give to the poor.
Love the Lord your God with all your being.

16

A Date with God

A Jewish traveler was stripped of his clothing, beaten, and left half dead alongside the road. Two Jewish religious leaders saw the man and walked on the other side of the road. Finally, a Samaritan, a man with whom the Jewish people had no relationship, was on his way to do his business saw the traveler and took pity on him." Luke 10:25–37 The Good Samaritan, a story shared by Jesus.

As I rushed up to the stop light, I saw a lady sitting on the pavement. She held her newborn baby in one hand and in the other hand she held a sign. I didn't know what was on the sign and today I didn't care. I couldn't stop. With my feet moving at lightning speed I dashed through the pedestrian crossing.

I looked back. I shouldn't have if I wanted to remain blind to the woman and her baby. The baby smiled at me, and I watched her longer than I should have. Her smile disrupted my plans and reminded me that she was loveable, human, and deserves my attention. I hesitated in the middle of the crosswalk, but I allowed the six seconds on the amber stop light to dictate my next steps. I rushed to the other side of the road heading to my destination... the

Jehovah Rohi – God is Our Lord

train and then home.

The unexpected was upon me, and I felt compelled to rush back to the woman and her baby. The strong urge pulled at my heart to go back, but I succumbed to my needs to rush home to my own family. I tried to quiet my loud and chatty conscience, so I told myself – "I cannot save the world." "This one is for someone else."

I stopped to see if anyone was giving her money; generosity from others would have released my guilty conscience. But like me, no one offered any help. NO ONE STOPPED. NOT ONE PERSON.

The routines of our lives are like waves, carrying us away from our humanity and we lose sight of the awesomeness of God in each other. Bit by bit we lose the connection that binds us together, the reason for all the suffering we see around us.

The pace of our lives must be interrupted for us to be reconnected to each other, to the God that resides in our sisters and brothers. Sometimes it is an illness, other times financial loss, that day it was the baby's smile that interrupted the speed of my routine.

People were moving like leaves in the wind, walking mindlessly, minding their own business. They had eyes but couldn't see. What would it take to open their eyes?

The lady with her sign and the smiling baby stood out like the lone tree on a deserted island. Still, they were invisible.

******

Jehovah Rohi – God is Our Lord

I could hear the train rumbling, and I ran down into the belly of the train station. As I was about to enter the gate, I felt another tug on my heart, and this time it was more than a tug this time I could hear God's voice –

"Where are you going? "You have unfinished business."

I looked up at the sign signaling the trains' arrival; the next train was three minutes.

"Are you going to abandon me by the roadside?"

"I am not abandoning you, God."

"I am the woman at the side of the road. I am the baby in her arms.

I abandoned my plans; going home on time was no longer my priority. I have a date with God. I retraced my steps, ran back up the steps and I watched again as each pedestrian passed that lady. I saw me in each person who passed by with their heads held high, and I surrendered to the Divine.

"O God you have been preparing me for this moment since 6:30 this morning."

April 21, 2017, I woke up with the prayer on serenity on my mind -

"O Divine Master, grant that I may not so much seek to be consoled as to console; to be understood, as to understand; to be loved, as to love; for it is in giving that we receive, it is in pardoning that we are pardoned, and it is in dying that we are born to Eternal Life.

Jehovah Rohi – God is Our Lord

******

I ran across the road, tears streaming, ugly crying and I fell on my knees on the sidewalk, I rested my head on her shoulder, and asked the lady to forgive me. How could I have ignored God because He was a poor woman? How Could I have ignored God because He was a helpless baby?

What happened next was supernatural, as long as I was on my knees praying and talking with this lady people came up and gave her money. For about five minutes nonstop there were Good Samaritans who offered her cash. Not only did they handed her cash they stopped and talked with her.

One man - *"please accept this; this is all I have."* Another man, *"I am a young father, and I understand how difficult it is."*

Here I am in the middle of Washington D.C. dressed in executive work suit, on my knees with my head on the shoulder of a woman begging by the roadside. She was comforting me and telling me that God loves me and that she will pray for me. We see God and feel the power of His undiluted love when we connect as human beings.

******

Could it be that one person can make a difference? Could it be that you and I can be the fire that stokes the conscience of others?

Could we cause the eyes of others to open and see the suffering around us, and the beauty in all humanity?

Could it be that we can be the light that eradicates

darkness?

I almost missed the face of God on April 21, 2017.

I have read the story of the Good Samaritan over and over and each time I've quietly said to myself –

"I would be the Good Samaritan."

"I could never pass someone in need."

******

As I look back on my life's journey, I was more often the Jewish religious leaders, caught up with my situations, my deadlines, my needs, and my intended destination that I lose sight of opportunities to be the Good Samaritan.

More importantly, when we walk away from the poor and needy, we miss the chance to look into the face of God.

******

Jehovah Rohi – God is Our Lord

Whatever we do to the poor we do to God – It is written in Matthew 25 verses 35 – 40. *"For I was hungry, and you gave me something to eat, I was thirsty, and you gave me something to drink, I was a stranger and you invited me in, I needed clothes, and you clothed me, I was sick and you looked after me, I was in prison and you came to visit me."   Then the righteous will answer him, "Lord, when did we see you hungry and feed you, or thirsty and give you something to drink?   When did we see you a stranger and invite you in, or needing clothes and clothe you?   When did we see you sick or in prison and go to visit you?"   The King will reply, "Truly I tell you, whatever you did for one of the least of these brothers and sisters of mine, you did for me."*

******

Miracles happen when we obey the voice of God.
Miracles happen when we love our neighbors.
Miracles happen when we let go of self.
Miracles happen when humans connect.

God Sanctifies

Jehovah-M'Kaddesh

**Jehovah who Sanctifies – He sets us apart unto Himself
"..who has saved us and called us with a holy calling, not
according to our works, but according to His own purpose and
grace which was granted us in Christ Jesus from all eternity." 2
Timothy 1:9**

17

God Pursued Me in the Depths of My Sin

He restores my soul; He leads me in the paths of righteousness, for His name sake. Psalm 23 verse 3

I met God when I was at my worse. I was planning to turn my back on the most beautiful gifts that God had given me, my marriage, and my children. I was wrapped up in pain and loss, shame, pride, and my ego had gotten the best me. I thought about me more than I was thinking about my family. Instead of fixing the broken pieces of my life I wanted to discard everything, even the parts that filled me with joy.

The destructive force of my decisions was not lost on me. God had imprinted on my heart the tsunami effect leaving my marriage would have on my husband, my children, families and friends, and even me. The picture of my future wasn't just bleak; it was extremely dark should I choose to walk away.

Every decision we make goes into a time we are yet to see but will meet. I've read Proverbs 14 verse 1 – *Every wise woman builds her house, but a foolish one tears it down with her own hands.* Who knew that I would be the foolish woman?

******

While God was pursuing me to give me the abundant life, evil was pressuring me into building a temple of doom. The Bible tells us, *"For our struggle is not against flesh and blood, but against the rulers, against the authorities, against the powers of this world's darkness, and against the spiritual forces of evil in the heavenly realms."* Ephesians 6 verse 12.

I was a walking turmoil, good and evil struggled within me:

"You deserve a better life. Imagine all the fun you will have if you leave Mark and the children."

"What God joined man should not separate."

"You got married too young and never got to see the world." "Don't you know you deserve some fun and freedom?"

"I came that you might have life and have life more abundantly. I have been directing your life and have blessed you."

"You are already on the path; you have no choice but to commit. Pack your bags and leave! Do you think that God wants you?"

"I will never leave you nor forsake you."

"Who do you think you are? Are you better than the people in your community? The abundant life is not for you? You are a sinner! You are not good enough!"

"Do not fear, for I have redeemed you. I have called

Jehovah M'Kaddesh – God Sanctifies

you by your name. You are Mine"

Evil is persuasive. At first, it uses slick words, painting a beautiful picture that all will be well when you choose the destructive path. If you resist, evil uses shame to force you on a path of destruction. Be aware of these tactics.

Evil conquered me for a few years because I believed the lie that God couldn't love me because I was not perfect. I thought to myself – "I am so bad already I might as well commit to the dark path that I was walking. There is no good left in me." I made several devastating decisions, and I had taken a mouthful of my version of the poisoned apple.

******

God is love and is never about shaming or forcing you to choose Him. The very presence of God will disrupt your evil ways and creates a hypersonic awareness of good and evil. However, God always leaves us to choose. What I know is that receiving God's material gifts doesn't mean that we will turn to the Giver of good gifts. Look at my life.

God took me out of the ghetto and from extreme poverty. My entire life is a miracle in motion: how I finished college, how I got my first job, as I'm thinking about my life now, all my jobs were a result of divine acts. If my life was a book and you flipped through the chapters, you could see God's hand at work stitching the pieces together. But along the way, I lost sight of God's love and His ways. I was no longer worshipping the Creator; instead, I worshipped the created. A most dangerous place to be and I lived in that dangerous place.

*****

1998, during the time I was planning the great escape from my marriage, I had my third miscarriage and had a Dilation and Curettage (D&C) operation. Between waking up and being in the semi-conscious state, I met God. God placed me in that hospital bed where I could be still, to see Him, and to feel His love.

In God's presence, all I could feel was incredible love. I am incompetent with words that could sufficiently describe God's love for me. The love I felt was intense; it covered me, all of me. God's love filled me with perfect light. God's love could not be measured, and it could not be contained in the room. It is the kind of love that makes me want to be good without being told how bad I was. There was no judgment in God. Perfect love has no judgment.

******

Perfect love is truth and God stepped aside so that I could get the full view of my life. I saw the dangerous road that I was taking. I became aware of all the wrongs I was committing, the pains and sufferings that I had never surrendered. My life was in focus and living colors. The picture God showed me was this –

My sins were in a large crocus (burlap) bag in the corner of the hospital room. The bag looked lifelike but was motionless. I could see the outline of the items in the bag; they were all shapes and sizes. The bag looked to be

Jehovah M'Kaddesh – God Sanctifies

about 8 feet long and 4 feet wide, and if I had guessed the weight, I would say it weighed about 1,000 pounds. I carried that around for a long time thinking I had no option, shamed by evil's cunning.

******

Can I tell you something about sin? Listen to me, sin grows from the wounds of our past, and we are incompetent to heal those wounds by ourselves. Without the love of God in us, we will inflict the pain we carry on the people we love. We can only give to others what we have and if hurt is all we have then hurt is what we will share. We need Jesus to help us. Without the knowledge and wisdom of our Father God, we will create wounded generations.

I was surprised to learn that I was carrying the pains that others had inflicted on me. We are the product of what we have done willingly and what others did to us. Why should I bear the weight of the sins that others commit against me? But that was what I did for years.

******

I have asked for forgiveness of my sins before but never surrendering all. Total surrender was difficult for me; I had a skewed understanding of God's love. I thought I had to be perfect. I figured out from my relationship with family members and friends that to receive their love I had to be perfect, and I placed God in the same category. As a child, I received love and attention whenever I worked hard, and I was working hard to win His love, but I could

Jehovah M'Kaddesh – God Sanctifies

not keep up with the work, and so I gave up on God and right living.

Also, I didn't know that I needed to surrender all the hurt and pain from my past, not only the wrongs I did, but harm inflicted on me by others. I had no clue that the things I saw, heard, and felt as a child and young adult had produced in me some of the wrongs I was committing. It is in complete surrender that we get total healing.

I needed healing from harsh words that pierced my heart over the years, the lack of love from people who I thought should have loved me, abuse from people who should have cared for me, the neglect I felt fending for myself. I saw that I was filled with hate, rage, and bitterness for those who never had what was necessary to love me and care for me.

I also needed healing from the hurts I have caused. The harsh words I had spoken to others, displacement of my time and efforts, fornication, and lies. My past might have created the path I took, but I voluntarily choose to walk those pathways into sin.

I have sinned against God and walked away from His Banner of love. I needed cleansing, and I needed the love and peace that comes with being a child of God. How could God love me so much with all the wrong things I have committed? Who could love me so deeply?

I was broken. And for the first time in my life, I knew for sure that I couldn't make it on my own. There were no sacrifices, no perfect works that could make me whole. I

Jehovah M'Kaddesh – God Sanctifies

knew that I needed Jesus. I wept with the knowledge of how deep I was in sin and still God was pursuing me to show me His massive, unmeasurable love.

******

I acknowledged the bag and its contents. I was expecting God to take each item piece by piece from the bag and question me about them. But instead of throwing my sins in my face and pointing out each one, God separated my wrongs from me and showered me with so much love.

Next, God stood between me and my sins and God spoke to me –

"I love you. You are perfect. I made you for good works. You are light. Follow me."

The voice was sweet and soft; it felt like a pillow that could give me rest. I said yes to following God. It took me several years after this experience to fully surrender all parts of my life to God.

I had to write this experience down quickly; I wanted to capture the intensity of God's love. I was still weak and was disoriented and fell off the bed. I was still hooked up to the intravenous drip, but I needed to write. I wandered around the room, rolling the drip stand behind me. I found a yellow note pad and pencil, and I wrote –

"Today I went to heaven, and I was surprised to see I was still the child God wanted me to be. He gave me a heart as pure as gold. He washed me with His love and made me whole. Today I went to heaven and I was surprised to see God had my future planned for me, it was great, it was grand, too much that I could not stand. Today I went to heaven and I was in God's hands."

I knew I had the choice of either picking up that package, becoming its slave and destroying myself and those who cared for me. Or I could choose to walk in the light that God used to bathe me and experience abundant joy and peace. I choose the light and so can you. I cried out to God to save me, to deliver me from my past. I cried out for a new heart because I had a lot of forgiving to do and a lot to seek. God heard me and has been sanctifying me ever since.

My singing is horrible. But in that room, I made melody singing:

"All to Jesus I surrender. All to Him I freely give. I will ever love and trust Him. In His presence daily live. All to Jesus I surrender. Humbly at His feet I bow. Worldly pleasures all forsaken. Take me, Jesus, take me now. I surrender all. I surrender all. All to Thee my blessed Savior." (Judson W. Van DeVenter, 1896)

The devil tells us barefaced lies and we believe them – we are that one wrong thing that we have done – the lies we told, the things we stole, the abortions we had, the strange beds we find ourselves in, the children we fathered while married, the children we knowingly gave to the wrong man, the hate we felt, the lives we took. We are none of those

Jehovah M'Kaddesh – God Sanctifies

things. Turn your back on those lies and surrender to Love.

You are light! Embrace that light you will be amazed that you can drop that package of guilt and shame. You can live in God's love. Jesus said, in Matt 11:28-29 *"Come unto me, all ye that labor and are heavy laden, and I will give you rest. Take my yoke upon you and learn of me; for I am meek and lowly in heart: and ye shall find rest unto your souls."*

I left that package in that hospital on Brandon Hill Road in Montego Bay. Have I been tempted to pick it up again? Yes. Yes. Yes. But I have learned – *"Trust in the Lord with all my heart and lean not on my own understanding. In all my ways I have been acknowledging God and let Him direct my path."*

I believe that the healing process for my many ailments started the day I made a commitment to let go of the burdens I carried around for years. You can drop your package too and choose Christ today.

******

You are light.
You are Perfect.
You are loved just as you are.

Jehovah M'Kaddesh – God Sanctifies

Creator? All wisdom and knowledge come from the Divine. I am so happy that God sees the heart and pursues us until we learn the lessons that we must learn. Our thoughts, words, and actions reveal the condition of the heart, and my heart needed a transformation.

King David wrote in 1 Chronicles 29 verse 12 - *"Wealth and honor come from You; You are the ruler of all things."* Everything comes from God. However, I was reluctant to invest what He had graciously left in my guardianship in the manner that would result in the highest rate of return. His instructions were clear, never leaving anything up to my imagination.

"Every month put the $__ in an envelope. No one should know what you are doing, only the person who delivers the envelope. Ms. Laine should never know about your involvement."

In the book of Matthew, chapter 6 verse 8 Jesus said, *"your Father knows what you need before you ask Him."* God knew what Ms. Laine needed, and He also knew that I needed clear instructions to do His will.

******

I told Mark, what I had to do, and he agreed. Every month I placed the money in an envelope, gave it to my close friend, and she carried out the secret mission. While I was planning my move to the USA in 2004, God reminded me that distance did not release me of my obligations. I arranged with my friend to continue the monthly payments as God had directed me.

Jehovah M'Kaddesh – God Sanctifies

******

In 2007 I made a surprise trip home. No one in Jamaica knew that I would be home, not even my parents. Imagine my utter amazement when I approached my childhood home, and I saw Ms. Laine sitting on the verandah.

Ms. Laine got word that the money was coming from one of Brother Bell's daughters and she came to bless her. She thought it was my eldest sister, Marvia, who had left for the store just minutes before Ms. Laine arrived. My parents didn't know what I had been doing for Ms. Laine over the last four years, but when Ms. Laine explained to them why she was visiting they suspected that I was the one helping. Now, they were conflicted and didn't know what to tell Ms. Laine. Mama said, "God knows best so if Marvia gets the blessings that is how it should be." My parents had no plans to intervene.

When I walked through the gates, I got the reaction I hoped for, everyone was delighted and shocked to see me. Mama ran to greet me, wrapping her arms around my neck. Dada stood by the metal gate on the verandah with a broad grin etched across his face. My heart raced as I stepped up to greet Ms. Laine –

"Ms. Laine, how are you?" What are you doing these days?"

"Me awright." "Me come fi bless yu sista but she gone a shop." "God send me fi bless har."

I didn't know what to do. Should I come clean and

Jehovah M'Kaddesh – God Sanctifies

confess, or should I allow my sister to get the blessings? God had commanded me to keep this a secret. I always knew I struggled with pride and had often asked God to cleanse me of my prideful ways. Now, this. What if my pride resurfaced?

******

"Kneel before her and confess. It is time."

I knelt in surrender to the Divine, a most beautiful, terrifying, powerful, and humbling experience. Yes, I still had pride, I could feel it in my heart, the way my knees hesitated to fall before a humble handmaid of God. But before God, *"every knee will bow, and every tongue will confess..."* Romans 10 verses 10-12. I fell on my knees and surrendered my pride.

"Ms. Laine, I am the one who sent the money to you. How did you find out?" She couldn't recall who told her.

I was revealing myself on God's terms. Not my own. I wasn't snapping photos of my good deeds for my friends to see but on my knees before God and His servant, Ms. Laine. 1 Peter 5 verse 6 tells us – *"Humble yourselves, therefore, under God's mighty hand, so that in due time He may exalt you.*

I was about to find the beauty and power in humility when a servant of the Divine honored me. There were no shining lights, no applause from well-dressed onlookers, there were no other contenders, and I wasn't standing on a stage beaming with pride. I was in my parents' humble

Jehovah M'Kaddesh – God Sanctifies

home, surrounded by my Mama, Dada, and Ms. Laine, all dressed in poor man's yard clothes. I was on my knees, clutching my chest, a swift surgical pain swept through my heart relieving me of pride that I was too proud to admit I had hidden there. Tears streamed down my face. Ms. Laine placed her hand on my head and prayed God's blessings upon me. I thought I went home to surprise my parents, but God was preparing a surprise for me.

******

When God first told me to share my blessings with Ms. Laine, and I complained, I had no idea that God was setting me up for my rewards. That morning in 2003, when I looked in the mirror I had failed to see the woman that God was making out of me. The love of money, the pride of life, and self-centricity disconnect us from God's grace and salvation. But God is so merciful that He pursues us despite our evil ways.

The blessings from Ms. Laine wasn't one of material wealth but a surgical transformation of my heart and a renewing of my mind. Her prayer implanted a GPS that continually directs me to God – the center of my life. I now have a barometer, reminding me to love my neighbor as myself. I now have a Richter scale that alerts me when I am too focused on the created things instead of the Creator of all things.

Your transformation is one obedient action away. Who God loves He pursues, and I know that you are on His list.

Jehovah M'Kaddesh – God Sanctifies

"For I know the plans I have for you," declares the Lord, "plans to prosper you and not to harm you, plans to give you hope and a future. Jeremiah 29 verse 11

******

God honors those who honors Him.
All wealth and power belongs to God.
Treat the poor with dignity.
God never blesses us for ourselves.

Jehovah M'Kaddesh – God Sanctifies

God is Everywhere

Jehovah El Roi

The God who sees me
Romans 8:38-39 "For I am sure that neither death nor life,
nor angels nor rulers, nor things present nor things to come,
nor powers, nor height nor depth, nor anything else in all
creation, will be able to separate us from the love of God in
Christ Jesus our Lord."

19. Prison Bars Cannot Keep God Away
20. Even in Death We Are Not Alone (Angels to Take Us
    Home)

19

Prison Bars Cannot Keep God Away

"Blessed be the God and Father of our Lord Jesus Christ, the Father of mercies and God of all comfort, who comforts us in all our affliction so that we will be able to comfort those who are in any affliction with the comfort with which we ourselves are comforted by God." 2 Cor. 1:3-4

Tears rolled down my cheeks as I dialed my sister's number. Nothing could soothe the severe damage in my heart. My pain was deep as it was enormous. Even I could not comprehend the depths of my own sorrow.

Do you know what it is like to lose a sibling? If you have never lost a loved one let me tell you and hope you never have to endure such loss. If you have, I'm sorry for stripping the band aid off a terrible wound but what I will share with you may lessen your pain.

My brother Mark passed away on March 31, 2006. His death was a sudden earthquake that measured 10 on my Richter scale. A volcanic eruption that demolished my heart and left me in a constant state of aftershocks. What I felt was not pain. The loss of a loved one is not pain; there

Jehovah El Roi – God is Everywhere

must be another name for what the living feels in the after-death. It is the violent separation of a body part I had but never knew existed. Nothing anyone could say or do could ease the pain. Nothing could fill the hole in my heart.

Dead at a tender age of 33. Mark didn't even live to have grey hairs on his head. He had young children, children he will never see as adults. His daughters will get married without him walking them down the aisle. Mark was the one who should sing amazing grace at our parent's funeral, and I watched as my parents mourned him. I cannot speak of my parents' pain, but I know my father never recovered and he died from a broken heart five years later.

******

I was inconsolable, and only my eldest sister's voice could provide temporary calm to my soul. It was Marvia who cared for us when we were little. Marvia washed, cooked, bathe us, and even dispense the occasional discipline. And now, all I needed is to hear her voice. Talking about our childhood temporarily erased the present. Somehow our lives always seem more impressive when it is in the past, even the sorrows we had endured seemed like light afflictions, ones not too heavy to carry in the present.

I lived for those chats with Marvia, somedays we didn't even reminisce we would only cry. Let me tell you, crying by yourself is not as good as crying with someone else. My husband could not comfort me. What does he know of my brother? It wasn't his brother. He had never

Jehovah El Roi – God is Everywhere

lost a brother so what could he tell me? That he understood my pain? No, he couldn't. Only a sister could help me through this rough patch. Only a sister knows the depths of my pain; only a sister felt what I was feeling.

******

Thursday, May 4, 2006. I dialed my sister's number, but I didn't hear her voice. The person on the other end answered and it was a male. My mind was in a state of constant loss, and it took me to the deep end. Someone had kidnapped my sister, and maybe she was dead. My tears dried up, I panicked. Did someone kill Marvia and took her phone? What now! Terror rose in my throat. I tried to stay calm. I needed to be kind to this man if he has my sister and hasn't yet taken her life; my kindness might encourage him to release her. I cannot look in the face of another loss.

I asked for my sister –

"May I speak to Marvia?"

The gentleman asked –

"Miss, are you an angel?"

He is trying to drive me crazy. Didn't he hear my question? What has he done? I looked at my phone screen and double checked the number I had dialed, and it is my sister's number.

******

Something is wrong. I was about to hang up the phone and I heard –

"Ask him if he knows Jesus?"

Jehovah El Roi – God is Everywhere

"Do you know Jesus?"

He answered with the question again –

"Miss, are you an angel?"

"No, but I know Jesus."

Tiny sobs dripped through the phone.

"Miss yu know where yu call?"

"No but I was trying to call my sister."

"Miss me inna prison."

I wasn't about to ask how he got a phone in lockup.

"Miss, dis morning when me wake up me ask God if Him real fi send me an angel. Just send me someone fi talk to about life." "Miss, prison lonely and dark yu know."

We spoke for 30 minutes or more, and I shared with him my experiences of God's love. I shared some of my life's struggles with him and how God worked miracles in my life. I listened to his life's stories and the hopes and dreams he had for himself.

I was crying now but not out of my loss but out of joy. No matter where you are or what you have done God cares about you and he will take a misdialed number to reach His son in prison to let him know that He (God) loves him and cares for him.

It is not about me. The pain of my brother's death did not go away but it was no longer my focus and so it was less intense. "Turn your eyes on Jesus, look into His wonderful face, and the things of the earth will go strangely dim the light of His glory and grace." I've sung this song a

Jehovah El Roi – God is Everywhere

thousand times or more, but I didn't know the meaning until May 4, 2006. The face of Jesus is our brothers and sisters in need. When we help those in need, the intensity of our problems dissipate.

Two miracles took place that Thursday morning –

God showed His son in prison that he was loved and that He (God) is near to him. Romans 8:38-39 *"For I am sure that neither death nor life, nor angels nor rulers, nor things present nor things to come, nor powers, nor height nor depth, nor anything else in all creation, will be able to separate us from the love of God in Christ Jesus our Lord."*

And as for me, that was the last day I was compelled to call my sister to cry and mourn the loss of my brother. I realized that God is the Comforter and He is with me. We will not forget our struggles, but we must remember, *"sorrow may come in the night, but joy comes in the morning."* Psalm 30:5.

There are days when I've asked –

"God, do you care for me?"

In May 2018 I was feeling sad, and I prayed to God for comfort. Within minutes of praying the Administrative Assistant came rushing to my office,

"Oh, Gwen" she exclaimed, "I just came to give you a hug."

All I needed was a hug, and God sent someone who doesn't know the desires of my heart to give me a hug.

Jehovah El Roi – God is Everywhere

2 Corinthians 12:9-10 - But he said to me, *"My grace is sufficient for you, for my power is made perfect in weakness."* *Therefore, I will boast all the more gladly of my weaknesses, so that the power of Christ may rest upon me. For the sake of Christ, then, I am content with weaknesses, insults, hardships, persecutions, and calamities. For when I am weak, then I am strong.*

******

Life is not all about us.
We cannot out-sin God's love for us.
Nothing can separate you from God's love.
When you help the oppressed you are honoring the Divine.

Even in Death We Are Not Alone
(Angels to Take Us Home)

"When they saw him, they worshiped him; but some doubted. Then Jesus came to them and said, "...Surely, I am with you always, to the very end of the age." Matthew 28 verse 20

"Gigi, the angels have Grandpa." The startling beauty of the words from this tiny boy jolted us from our mourning. Our tears evaporated without effort. We looked intensely at the blank wall where he pointed hoping to catch a glimpse of what he saw.

Rori, our six-year-old son, came face to face with the other side of life. He confirmed what Jesus told His disciples in Matthew 28 verse 20, *"surely, I am with you always, to the very end of the age."* This means even in death God is with us.

******

His death wasn't a surprise. We received the cancer diagnosis four weeks before, and on September 8th he told us four days were all he had left. Four days that would transform the lives of everyone who saw him exhaled one last time and everyone who sat in the weeping circle.

******

Maas Lloydie, that's what I called him. His friends called him Shago. His real name is Lloyd Norbert Kameka. The grandson of German immigrants who came to Jamaica seeking a better life. He stood six feet four inches tall, built like a warrior, with herculean shoulders, and strong hands. His eyes were sparkling blue as if God had dipped them in the Caribbean Sea.

His good looks never handed him any favors, at least from his stepfather. His status at birth denied him the right to a last name and the privilege of an education. Lloyd was kept at home to help with chores around the yard until he was considered old enough to work for a living. Before he was fourteen, he worked in the fields to provide for his younger siblings.

He was brilliant, could have been an excellent engineer only if he was given the opportunity. His plight is that of many boys in Jamaica, black, brown or white. There is no discrimination when it comes to boys on the island taking on manhood before the time was right.

******

Age and illness erased the once splendid man, but, if you looked long enough, you could have caught a glimpse of what he was in former years. He was still handsome, and he had the grasp of strength in his hands. His blond hair had turned shocking silver-white with stray strands constantly wandering against his creased forehead dusted with age spots.   He would slick back his hair with weathered hands that showed signs of age, hard labor, and the harsh Jamaican sun.   Whatever ailed him made him bowlegged removing a few inches from his towering height. He was slightly hunched over and used a stick to support his weight. It pained me to watch him move about the yard. He walked with a tortured limp with excessive emphasis on his left leg.   Maas Llyodie worked the fields even in his late sixties, tackling tasks too difficult for his age.

Maas Lloydie was etched deep from the block of Catholicism, but he displayed no signs of being religious, and he never spoke of the mysteries of the spiritual realm. He never went to church but was happy to see his wife attend.   It was her duty to provide all the details of the church service – the songs, the lesson preached, the communion. He listened with deep intent, but he had no intention of going there himself. As far as I am concerned, he was a man of four dimensions:

He was a husband - with an acute depth of love for his wife. I've never heard him said 'I love you' to his wife. But it was evident in the way he playfully slapped her butt every time she walked by him and how he reminisced on the first time that he laid eyes on her.   He was a great provider, he didn't have much, but he gave all he had. Sometimes his jobs would take him far away from home for months. He always returned home.

He was a father - who displayed unbridled devotion to

Jehovah El Roi – God is Everywhere

his children, four sons, and a daughter. He didn't teach them anything, but they learned everything from him. Can I tell you? He raised men who nurture their children and cherish their wives. Men who can wrestle a cow to the ground one minute and the next minute they are singing nursery rhymes to toddlers. I was fortunate to marry one of his four sons.

He was a grandfather - with fierce compassion for his grandchildren. He was very gentle with his grandbabies. All 16 grandchildren who knew him adored him. And those born after his death learned of his legendary ways. Skilled at solving puzzles, he taught them the magic in the deck of cards, and his ability to make them giggle.

By 1996 his legs couldn't carry him anymore, and he moved around the house on a wheelchair. While he missed the ability to help his wife with chores this never dampened his spirit. He took the grandchildren on joy rides around the house on his wheelchair. Who could forget the days when he sat patiently while his granddaughters plaited his silver-white hair and decorated his head with colorful clips as if he was their doll. He sang to them –

"You are my sunshine, my only sunshine. You make me happy when skies are gray. You'll never know dear, how much I love you. Please don't take my sunshine away."

He was proud but not with his grandchildren; at least he wasn't with my daughter. He would ask her to read the Bible to him, a request that puzzled her.

Jehovah El Roi – God is Everywhere

"Gigi, come read de Bible fi me."

"But Grandpa, you can read it yourself."

"Me can't see de writing, dem too small."

"Grandpa, it is the same as the newspaper and you read the newspaper every day."

Marjanne, (Gigi) would eventually read the Bible to her grandfather. She filled a space that no one knew he had, a longing to hear the word of God. And he held on to his secret, his desire to decipher the written words.

A builder of community, knowledge bearer, and jack of all trades - he built homes, he farmed the land, he restored sick animals to health, he invented tools and repaired old equipment, and he prepared the dead for burial. His oratorical skills coupled with his knowledge of the news in Jamaica and around the world drew the men from neighboring communities to his home. They sat around him in the evenings as he gave a blow by blow account of the news. He juxtaposed current events with the past, carefully phrasing each word so that the common man had an unclouded vision of what he wanted them to know. He was a great speaker but a better listener with unparalleled memory.

******

Our first meeting was a fierce battle. Mark has no such recollection - children must create the parents they want, and so he erased the memories of that day in October 1989. I remembered his machete, his wife's sticks, the derogatory words used to describe my color and my integrity, and the stones that I picked up to defend myself.

My black skin must have dragged him back to painful memories, a recollection of his identity, the part everyone tried to ignore. We called a silent truce months later because of our shared love for Mark. That's another story, I promise to share.

******

He was 79 years old when we found out that Dr. Tannor had misdiagnosed his ailment. Refractory multiple myeloma was treated as arthritis for two years. A broken arm from simply raising himself from a bench opened the grave reality of his condition. He wore an orthopedic cast on his arm for three months, and when the doctor removed the cast, the bone in his arm had crumbled. Dr. Francis, the bone specialist, did the blood test and revealed what we already suspected. Cancer, the dreaded C had ravished his body. The x-rays showed his bones were porous, paper thin. Cancer had demolished his bones and was slowly destroying his organs.

******

September 7, 1999 was the start date for his chemotherapy. Mark picked him up from his home in Seaford Town. Seaford Town is approximately twenty-five miles from the hospital in Montego Bay, and where two of his children lived, Mark and his daughter Lorna. On the way to the hospital, he resigned from the doctor's orders –

"Chemo don't mek no sense yu know Markie. Oonu no badda waste oonu money. No carry me a no hospital, me ready fi go home."

"Daddy, you sure? Why don't you give this doctor a try?"

"Markie me live a good life. Me ready fi go. Tek care a Mary fi me."

He was sure of his condition, and he insisted that we take him to his daughter's home. Maas Llyodie almost sounded prophetic –

"Markie, me no want fi dead inna no hospital and me no want fi give oonu no trouble fi bring me body back to MoBay. Take me to Lorna's house. Me only have four more days yu know."

Even in the face of death, he wasn't concerned about himself. Many people nearing death want to die in their bed. Maas Llyodie didn't want to be a burden in life neither in death. Mark obliged.

******

How does one prepare for his death? I do not know if there is a plan written on our hearts how this should unfurl. However, I will share with you Maas Lloydie's journey. It lasted four days and 17 hours after he resigned from his doctor's care – 10 AM September 7, 1999, to 5 AM September 11, 1999.

******

Tuesday, September 7th – Day 1 Music and Prayers

We took him to his daughter's home, as he requested. He asked Mark to play him gospel songs. Mark created a cassette tape with some of his favorites:

Jehovah El Roi – God is Everywhere

"Coming soon Jesus in all his glory."
"This world is not my home."
"Take my hand precious Lord."
"It is no secret what God can do."
"I cross the bridge, there will be no sorrow."
"I'd rather have Jesus than silver or gold."

His love for God was on display, the side of him I never knew or never bothered to recognize. Each one of us is deeper and more complex than the naked eye can see. A new man was being revealed to me, I watched him waving his hand to the beat of the music and I listened to his failing voice praising God. Cancer had broken his body, but it was still a temple fit for worship.

Could it be that in death a man is transformed or is it that death reveals the inner man? I believe that a man's ego cannot withstand the power of truth that comes with death. Death's strength exposes the wirings of the soul and the contents of the heart. Death reveals the essence of the man. Death's path has no space for pride. Death reveals our truths.

Dr. Francis had told us his pain would be severe, but there he was on his back preparing to leave his broken body, and he never complained, not even once.

He loved music, and Mark recalled the days his father sang to him –

"From this valley they say you are leaving. We shall miss your bright eyes and sweet smile. For you take with you all of the sunshine. That has brightened our

pathway a while. Then come sit by my side if you love me. Do not hasten to bid me adieu. Just remember the Red River Valley. And the cowboy that's loved you so true." (Marty Robbins - Red River Valley)

Mark wept. The song that once brought him comfort was now a source of sorrow. This song is a goodbye song, and he wasn't ready to say goodbye forever.

******

September 8th - Day 2 Prayers, Goodbyes, and Last Meal

His pain intensified, we knew because of the low groans that he couldn't stifle. Out of desperation, we asked Dr. Tannor to visit and to provide medication to ease the pain. Dr. Tannor refused both requests. Maas Lloydie suffered silently. He repeated the words we know were inevitable but didn't want to hear –

"No bother wid no medication, me only have three more days. Don't worry oonu self."

Our pain intensified, and there was no doctor to fix our broken hearts. We were trying to be hopeful and talked about taking him home,

"Me tell oonu, me only have three days fi live, don't mek no plans fi tek me back to Seaford Town."

******

His children had questions for which they needed answers. They needed to know about his life while he worked away from home and they also wanted to know the truth behind rumors that he fathered other children in the community –

"Daddy, so when you were working away from home you were gone for weeks. You didn't have any girlfriend?"

"Not really yu know. From me married Mary me no look pon nobady yu know. Before me meet yu mother, dis lady who cook fi me used to stop by, nothing serious."

"So Daddy, we have any brother or sister that you haven't told us about?"

"Well de lady had a likkle bwoy, and he was a stillbirth."

"Any more?"

"No more."

"What about Susan? Everybody says she looks like you."

No sah, me neva go deh soh, me neva trouble har mother."

The room erupted in laughter.

Maas Lloydie was brave, even in the face of death, he found the courage and desire to laugh. He was dying with a clean conscience, and he was surrounded by the love of his life, Ms. Mary, his children, grandchildren, in-laws, and good friends. He had surrendered all to God, even his pride.

******

He had no appetite but asked for cream soda. Mark

purchased several bottles. He only wanted one and drank the cold, sweet, clear liquid slowly. He savored every drop, his last meal.

Maas Lloydie asked to talk to his two sons living in the USA and all his relatives living abroad. He spent the day saying goodbyes. He shared cherished memories from his younger years with us; his smile widened when he talked about meeting his wife for the first time.

Weariness tugged at him as the day progressed, but he pulled through like a soldier on the battlefield. He welcomed everyone who visited and answered every phone call. He ended every conversation with, "me love yu, tek care a yuself."

******

Mark asked me to pray for Maas Lloydie. I knelt by his bed and asked him –

"Maas Lloydie, can I pray with you?"

"Yes Mitchelle, yes." He always pronounced my name with a 't.'

I held his good hand; it was cold and wet, and strong. He curled his fingers lovingly around mine, and I prayed with him. Daily prayers were part of the routine until the end.

******

September 9th – Day 3 Face to Face with Jesus and Final Words

"Jesus, turn around and let me see your face."

He said those words with such clarity we almost

Jehovah El Roi – God is Everywhere

thought he was talking to someone in the room. He must be hallucinating. Could he have seen The Christ? The certainty of his death was etched in time. He told us a day ago on September 8th.

He had three days left, but he has not started to 'travel'. A person on the deathbed is said to be traveling after losing consciousness and cannot communicate with the living, but they are still talking. My father told me about a man who had long conversations with his deceased father while he was 'traveling'.

People who are 'traveling' are never conscious. Maas Lloydie had clarity of mind. I bent over him to see if his eyes were open or if he was talking in his sleep. He was awake.

"Maas Lloydie, did you see Jesus?

He nodded in the affirmative.

"Maas Lloydie, did you see His face?

He nodded yes again.

His face shone brightly and seemed to be getting younger right before my eyes. He was smiling.

"What did He look like?"

Silence....

I was anxious to know what the dying sees but Maas Lloydie could not respond. He had spoken his last words.

The last eight words that graced my father-in-law's lips was the beginning of a spiritual ascendancy for me. It is a journey of which I am still in awe. On his deathbed, I found a fountain of life from which I perpetually sip. His death was the most powerful spiritual experience I've had. Jesus comes to comfort the dying; death is not a lonely road. Mass Lloydie's status in life as a poor farmer who lived a humble life did not deny him access to Jesus.

When Jesus said - "I am with you even to the end." There were no qualifiers.

Could it be that the death of our loved ones comes not to rob us of our joy but to give us pause to rejoice in life and to prepare us for the next phase of life's journey?

He communicated to us during that time, two blinks for yes and one blink for no. Sometimes by squeezing our hands.

I couldn't let go of those eight words. Christ is real and reveals himself to the dying.

******

September 10th – Day 4 "The Wait"

The gospel songs played in the background lending us calm in these turbulent times. The certainty of his death was upon us and any hope we had steadily slipped from our hearts.

Maas Llyodie laid on the bed, still and quiet. The only movements were the shifting of his eyes beneath the lids and the gentle rise and fall of his chest as he breathed. His breathing was more exhaling and less inhaling. Each time he exhaled he made a sound, "phew." His appearance changed: bowlegs had disappeared, his body was the horizontal version of a soldier standing at attention, he was straight as an arrow, his feet together, not splayed as one who had lost control of his body, his nose seemed straighter than usual, and the aged spots had faded.

We asked him questions, and he blinked: twice for yes and once for no.

"Maas Lloydie are you thirsty?"

"Blink blink."

"Maas Lloydie did you see Mamie (his mother)."

"Blink."

We wet his lips with cold water from a dripping rag.

I prayed, and he squeezed my fingers.

******

September 11th – It is finished. Death comes in the morning

5 AM Saturday, September 11, 1999. The bright light in the bedroom jolted my mother and me from our sleep. Instinctively I knew it was time.

Mark, his brother Patrick, his sister Lorna, and a few friends played dominoes throughout the night. The burden of Maas Lloydie's impending death robbed them of their sleep. I looked at them through the opened door. They had aged several years in the last four days. They looked like guards keeping watch over thin air. In futility, they watched throughout the night.

The morning was beautiful. The air was still. I caught the first ray of the disciplined sun gliding over the mountains. The shimmering moon edged lazily towards the sea leaving a hint of darkness in the sky. The moon lingered long enough to see the sun's smile before it entered someone else's goodnight.

Nature conspired to cover death's tracks as it entered the room. The sudden gush of wind rustled the leaves on the soursop tree, and the birds sang in a chorus created a beautiful distraction. Maas Lloydie exhaled more rapidly.

I pondered what words I should use to summon those who waited for the cry of death. I didn't need words. Mark caught a glimpse of my face as I peered into the morning's soul. I nodded as his eyes captured mine and Mark knew it was time.

Patrick his firstborn, Lorna his only daughter, and Mark, rushed through the door and went to their father's bed. I closed my eyes and prayed –

"God give them strength to face this day." Show us your love in a special way."

I heard them crying and pouring their love on him.

"Michelle, Michelle, come and pray for Daddy one last time."

My husband pleaded, his voice filled with sorrow, pain, and loss. His daddy, the once splendid man, was no more. Mark was shaking; the tremor was coming from deep inside of him, the place that has no name, the part of human body that science teachers cannot explain and never asked us to label in anatomy class, the place where true love lives, the place where humans connect on a spiritual level, the part of us that never dies. I wanted to hold him, but I restrained myself. Some experiences should not be shared.

Jehovah El Roi – God is Everywhere

"Mark, he doesn't need any prayers now. Just let him know you love him. Spend the last moments with him."

He was still breathing, and he could hear his children. He never lost consciousness. He never 'traveled'. Mark made him a promise –

"Daddy, Daddy, me ago take care a Mama, no worry Daddy. Mama is going to be alright."

Mark said he shed a single tear; it rolled down his left cheek. Comforted by the promise that Ms. Mary, the love of his life, would be alright. He exhaled one last time as the moon slipped through the clouds leaving a trail of yesterday behind.

******

Mark and Lorna gathered all the grandchildren and Ms. Mary and told them he had passed. We all piled on the floor in a circle and wept. Every tear had a meaning; every rounded sparkle of water that fell from our eyes was unique and precious as the gift he left each of us, his love. Tears flowed without effort, a symphonic display of our pain.

The room burned with our sorrow and the mystical bright blue light that hovered over Maas Lloydie's bed.

******

Angels Among Us

Rori pointed to the tiny square of wall between the windows and the door. The quiet certainty of his six-year-old voice interrupted our mourning.

"Gigi, the angels have Grandpa."

In the harshness of our pain we can find the sweetest

Jehovah El Roi – God is Everywhere

joy, but to find it we must be willing to believe in the things we might never see. We must have faith.

Nobody believed that the dead could see. Then imagine the surprise to know that the dead can feel.

"They are looking down at grandma and grandpa is crying." See, he has one tear rolling down his left cheek."

We saw nothing. Just the blank wall peering back at us. Rori was emphatic about what he saw, and he wanted us to see it too –

"Yes, the two angels have Grandpa. Grandpa stopped to look at Grandma. Look, look, they are leaving."

Our curiosity about what Rori saw vaporized our pain. Maas Lloydie's children who saw that last tear slid down his cheek believed. His cousins were accusing him of lying. He stood firm in what he saw. Adults shot questions at him:

"What did the angels look like?"

"Like my spit, white, and you can see through them."

The only suitable analogy his six-year-old mind could conjure up.

"Describe their wings? Are they big?"

"Who told you that all angels have wings?" "I did not see any wings. I only saw their faces."

No one except Rori saw the angels, but several of us saw the bright blue light that hovered over his deathbed. We have no explanation for the blue light that filled the

Jehovah El Roi – God is Everywhere

space above his bed. But I have one for the presence of the angels, Jesus promised us that He is with us, always, even to the very end.

Rori is now an adult, ever so often I have asked him if he remembered what he saw on that day and he said yes but does not want to discuss the details. His childlike innocence has gone; he questions what he saw and tries to find scientific reasons for seeing two angels taking away his Grandpa. But he has never denied that the angels were with his Grandpa at the end.

Will an angel come to take us at death? I cannot say. What I know is God pursues us to the end. It is up to us if we will welcome the Lover of our souls into our lives. We must have a relationship with the Divine before we exhale our final breath. How else can we die in peace? It is God who gives the peace that Maas Lloydie had on his deathbed.

Maas Lloydie's death is the pedagogy of my Christian faith, the teacher who keeps reminding me that you and I are eternal beings. It was his last four days that revealed another dimension of God's love; God is with us every step of our lives.

******

Even in death, you will never walk alone.

Jehovah El Roi – God is Everywhere

Acknowledgements

Many thanks to everyone of friends and family who read my testimonies on Facebook and encouraged me to write this book.

I am thankful for the early readers who offered helpful feedback. Special mention to Francisca Meity Prasetyani, Kayon Hutchinson, Dr. Howard Kea, and Sharon Hines.

Patrick Green, you are one of kind. You offered the true, genuine advice that I needed to push through the tough times. Thanks for being the first reader.

Tiffany Francis Hurd, you were my first pre-order. After that first sale I had no choice but to finish this project.

Mama Bell and Daddy Bell, you have taught me to believe in God and the power of His might. Daddy Bell, you are no longer here but I want to say thanks for those many Saturday mornings when pushed through our silliness and you taught us the word of God.

To my children:

Melissa and Samantha, thanks for your patience while your mommy tried her hands at writing, and for your encouragement. I also want to thank you for allowing me to share your story.

Rori, thank you for always challenging me to be

better and to be totally used up. Thanks for reminding me that I cannot measure who I am and who I am becoming with the tools of the past.

Marjanne, thanks for helping me to dig deeper into the emotions within the stories and for those encouraging phone calls.

And most of all, Mark; there aren't enough words to thank you for your patience and grace, for the hours you spent taking care of the home and our children while I wrote, for the hours you spent editing and giving me advice. Without you this book would never be published. You make me stronger, better, kinder, and you allow me to be authentic. I do not only love you I live you.

About the Author

Gwendolyn Bell-Kameka (Gwen) is an auditor by profession and works in Washington D.C. She is an award winning motivational speaker and story-teller. Gwen operates a nonprofit in Jamaica, helping families in need. This is Gwen's first published work. She lives with her husband, Mark, their twin daughters, and her mother in Maryland.

55196889R00134

Made in the USA
Columbia, SC
14 April 2019